QUARKXPRESS 8

ESSENTIAL SKILLS
for Page Layout and Web Design

KELLY KORDES ANTON AND JOHN CRUISE

Peachpit
Press

Essential Skills for Page Layout and Web Design
Kelly Kordes Anton and John Cruise

Peachpit Press
1249 Eighth Street
Berkeley, CA 94710
510/524-2178
510/524-2221 (fax)

Find us on the Web at www.peachpit.com
To report errors, please send a note to errata@peachpit.com
Peachpit Press is a division of Pearson Education

Project Editor: Susan Rimerman
Production Editor: Lisa Brazieal
Copyeditor: Peggy Nauts
Compositors: Kelly Kordes Anton, John Cruise
Indexer: Karin Arrigoni
Cover Design Mimi Heft
Cover Illustration: Gordon Studer
Interior Design: Chris Gillespie, Happenstance

ISBN–13: 978-0-321-61691-3
ISBN–10:   0-321-61691-X

9 8 7 6 5 4 3 2 1
Printed and bound in the United States of America

ACKNOWLEDGMENTS

THE AUTHORS WOULD LIKE TO THANK EVERYBODY AT PEACHPIT PRESS, including Susan Rimerman, Lisa Brazieal, Peggy Nauts, Mimi Heft, for their attention to detail in making sure the book reads well and looks perfect. In addition, we appreciate the technical assistance and review time of Trevor Alyn, Dan Logan, and Scott Wieseler from Quark, Inc.

To lend a real-world touch to discussions in this book, we borrowed sample QuarkXPress files from talented graphic designers and QuarkXPress loyalists Andrea Späth, Connie Robertson, and Hugh Enockson, all contracted by Terry Vitale of New West Publishing.

Finally, we'd like to thank each other for providing inspiration and information for this book and for projects we've worked on over the last 12 years.

This book is dedicated to Kelly's boys, Robert and Michael Anton, and John's daughter, Ryan Cruise.

—KELLY KORDES ANTON AND JOHN CRUISE

FOREWORD

THE FIRST VERSIONS OF QUARKXPRESS gave designers and page layout artists a whole new way to do their work. This new way was better and faster—but for folks who were used to doing pasteup on a light table, it took a little bit of getting used to. So, fittingly, early QuarkXPress books concentrated on helping people who were used to thinking in terms of galleys and X-ACTO knives to learn their way around a GUI.

Today's designers and page layout artists, however, are quite familiar with the mechanics of digital page layout, thank you very much. The meat-and-potatoes features have been there for years, and they really haven't changed all that much since they were introduced.

Until now, that is. The architects of QuarkXPress 8 have reworked the user interface with the explicit goal of making meat-and-potatoes tasks a little quicker, a little easier. Most of the old ways of doing things are still there, of course, but there are all kinds of new shortcuts and buttons—not for features you never use, but for things you do all the time. Some of the changes seem minor by themselves, but together they add up to a whole new kind of upgrade.

To go with that whole new kind of upgrade, here's a whole new kind of book for QuarkXPress. Rather than walking you through stuff you've known for 10 or 20 years, Kelly Kordes Anton and John Cruise decided to help you find all the fantastic little time-savers in QuarkXPress 8 and to start using them. With this book you can take advantage of their insight and expertise—and then start taking advantage of QuarkXPress 8.

—Dan Logan, QuarkXPress Product Manager, Quark, Inc.

CONTENTS

QuarkXPress 8

IN THE LAST 20 YEARS, QUARKXPRESS HAS EVOLVED from a desktop publishing tool for print to a multi-faceted publishing program that provides expert output to a variety of media. Using QuarkXPress 8, you can do everything from produce a handful of business cards printed with a color inkjet to press-ready PDF files to Web sites and interactive Flash files. But the real reason you use QuarkXPress is to make these things look cool. Back in the day, we heard that word often from Quark founder Tim Gill, who never lost focus on the importance of design tools.

The hallmark features of QuarkXPress—expert typography and precision item placement—are augmented today with automatic drop shadows, image editing, opacity, drawing tools, tables, and high-end typographic features for multilingual print and online publishing. Every new version of QuarkXPress has also introduced and enhanced productivity features, making it easier to use, faster, and more interactive. Multiple users can now simultaneously work with—and seamlessly update—the same content to produce print, Web, and Flash materials. The majority of QuarkXPress users, however, design self-contained pieces for print such as the layout shown in **Figure 1** (next page).

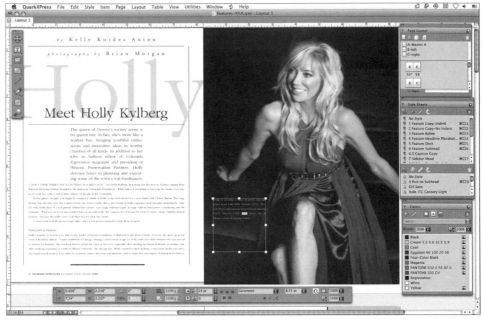

FIGURE 1: A magazine spread is typical of a QuarkXPress print piece. Commonly used layout aids include the tools at the left; the Measurements palette at the bottom, which provides quick access to all formatting features; and palettes for working with pages, styling text, and applying colors at the right.

The role of QuarkXPress

In publishing, QuarkXPress is generally considered an "end of the line" application, meaning that it's where the text and graphic files you work on in other programs ends-up. And it is, of course, where the content is output, whether in a print or online format. You can also create original content in QuarkXPress. It's always been a functional word processor, the drawing tools are much improved, and the image-editing tools are expanded in version 8. The cross-media capabilities make it possible for you to share content among print, Web, and Flash pieces, so the line now has more than one ending.

In most publishing workflows, however, content is created by experts in specialized programs. Writers produce copy in Microsoft Word, data is compiled in Microsoft Excel, digital images are fine-tuned in Adobe Photoshop, and logos and other graphics are created in Adobe Illustrator. All these pieces are pulled together in QuarkXPress, where you select typefaces and colors and design a layout to complement the content. Designers generally store all the pieces for a project in the same folder, as shown in **Figure 2.**

FIGURE 2: This folder contains typical pieces used in the creation of a brochure. In this case, the designer created the HockeyBrochure.qxp QuarkXPress project file to contain the print layout, imported the LeagueCopy.doc Word file containing the league descriptions, used the TeamRoster.xls Excel information in a table, and imported two image files: Player12.jpg and TeamLogo.eps. The designer also created a Fonts folder to store copies of the precise fonts used with the project (although the fonts themselves are activated through separate font management software).

Once in QuarkXPress, pieces usually come together in one of two ways—you can start with a predesigned template and plug in the pieces or design free-form from scratch, experimenting with various options. Either way, QuarkXPress puts many tools at your fingertips, including grids for aligning text and items; master pages that contain repeating design elements; item creation tools for drawing shapes and lines; typographic, image manipulation, and color options; expert handling of text, pictures, and tables; and professional print and online output.

Major publishers throughout the world use QuarkXPress for publishing books, newspapers, magazines, catalogs, direct-mail pieces, corporate communications, and much more. With the capabilities of QuarkXPress, a publisher might simultaneously produce multiple editions of a piece in multiple languages across multiple media. As you learn the basics of QuarkXPress 8, keep all this potential in mind— you never know when you may need it.

The building blocks of a QuarkXPress layout are the same regardless of the output media, and they've remained the same through every version of the program. Layouts consist of items (primarily boxes and lines) and contents (text and pictures), as shown in **Figure 3**. The ability to precisely organize and format items and contents is a hallmark of QuarkXPress.

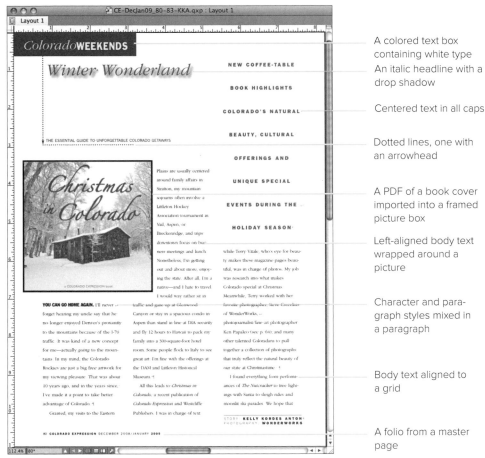

A colored text box containing white type

An italic headline with a drop shadow

Centered text in all caps

Dotted lines, one with an arrowhead

A PDF of a book cover imported into a framed picture box

Left-aligned body text wrapped around a picture

Character and paragraph styles mixed in a paragraph

Body text aligned to a grid

A folio from a master page

FIGURE 3: The building blocks of a QuarkXPress layout remain the same, whether this page is printed or accessed online.

Features in QuarkXPress that make this type of layout possible include:

- Predesigned master pages that contain repeating elements such as folios and text boxes for headlines (Chapter 9).

- The ability to create custom grids and guides for aligning items, pictures, and text (Chapter 9 and Chapter 5).

- Precision item placement, including rotation and scaling, with numeric and visual tools (Chapter 3).

- Drawing tools for creating boxes of any shape to contain color, text, and pictures (Chapter 3).

- Tools for creating lines, text paths, and tables (Chapter 2).

- Drag-and-drop text and picture import; integration with Adobe Illustrator, Photoshop, and Bridge (Chapter 7).

- The ability to create colors in all standard color models, including CMYK, RGB, PANTONE, and Web-Safe, and manage color for the best output across devices (Chapter 8).

- Options for experimenting with color and image transparency, layering, and image manipulation (Chapter 7 and Chapter 8).

- Drop shadows that can be applied to items, text, and images (Chapter 3, Chapter 5, and Chapter 7).

- High-end typography features, including built-in and custom hyphenation and justification settings, OpenType support, and hanging punctuation options (Chapter 5).

- The ability to create or import tables and apply formatting (Chapter 6).

- Word processing features such as search and replace, customizable spell check, and change case (Chapter 4).

- Item manipulation features such as item styles and item find/change (Chapter 3).

- Support for more than 30 languages, including East Asian languages.

- Familiar tools and interface for producing print, Web, and Flash content.

- The ability to share layouts and share content among layouts for collaboration and consistency.

- Expert output tools, including output styles, Job Jackets, and PDF/X support.

All these features come together in QuarkXPress to help you publish effectively and efficiently.

About this book

This book focuses on the primary tasks you'll perform in QuarkXPress while creating high-end print projects, and it helps you leverage those skills for use in Web and Flash publishing. We specifically targeted features that the average user needs to perform his or her daily work—in a real-world publishing environment. Each task included here is brief and self-contained, so you can quickly look up questions, skim the answers, and get back to work.

Since most users today either grew up with a computer or have been using one for more than a decade, we expect you to know how to:

- Start a program (Windows users) or launch an application (in Mac speak).

- Open, save, and close files—and then find them again. We're talking about any type of file, including the QuarkXPress files you create, digital image files you download or create, files received via e-mail, Word files, and so on.

- Consult experts as necessary on publishing topics such as expert typography, color, and high-end printing.

Although QuarkXPress lets you create print, PDF, Web, and Flash files, this book assumes print production. Information on PDF, Web, and Flash publishing is consolidated at the end of the book in Chapters 11 through 13. Otherwise, every task would be full of caveats about the differences in print and online workflows. In addition, the majority of basic features in QuarkXPress—creating boxes, formatting text, importing images—apply to both print and online workflows.

Learning the workspace

If you're new to QuarkXPress or desktop publishing in general, see Chapter 2 to orient yourself to the program. You'll learn about the main window that contains the pages you design; the general organization of the menus; the basic tools you need for creating and working with items, text, and pictures; and the floating palettes you'll use for everyday tasks. You'll also find out how to customize the workspace to suit your workflow and projects.

TIP **EXPERIMENT AND UNDO**

When learning new software and new features, experimentation is key. We encourage you to poke around in QuarkXPress and see what happens. You can undo just about every action, so it never hurts to click around and change settings while you're working and learning.

Retraining current users

Every previous version of QuarkXPress, particularly versions 3 through 7, looked basically the same. And they worked basically the same way, with new features basically tacked on and squeezed in. On the plus side, this allowed users to keep working as they had been, ignoring new features or learning them at their leisure. On the negative side, keeping everything the same led to a stagnant, inefficient interface.

QuarkXPress 8 introduces a whole new look and an entirely new, streamlined workflow. The software is similar enough that current users can hit the ground running—but different enough that they'll need to reorient themselves and learn the new features right away. If you're in this situation, head straight to the Retraining the QuarkXPress Mind appendix in the back of this book. Quark also provides a QXP What's New.pdf found in the QuarkXPress 8 > Documents > English folder.

For more information

Since QuarkXPress offers hundreds of options—and hundreds of tasks you might perform—this book does not cover everything. If you need to delve deeper into a feature, or learn about an advanced or special-purpose feature, check the resources provided with QuarkXPress.

Help and documentation

If you need information about a feature that is not covered in this book, try the Help file or the documentation provided with QuarkXPress. You will find the information surprisingly clear and helpful for documentation.

- **Help file:** Look in QuarkXPress Help for quick steps to perform a specific task. You can search for a specific task name, such as "hanging characters," or use the navigation tools.

- **User Guide:** To view the complete QuarkXPress 8 User Guide PDF file, navigate to this location: QuarkXPress 8 folder > Documents folder > English folder. The QXP User Guide.pdf folder provides complete workflow information that provides context and defines terms while explaining how to use each feature in QuarkXPress. You are not likely to want to print the 440-plus pages here, but you might think about moving the file to your desktop for quick reference.

- **Other resources:** In the same location as the User Guide, you'll find the QXP ReadMe.pdf, which provides information on system requirements, installing, and known issues. The QXP Troubleshooting.pdf is here as well, offering tips if the software is crashing or freezing, or if you're having printing or font issues. If you end up using XPress Tags, QuarkXPress formatting codes you can apply to text files, all the codes are in the XPress Tags Guide.pdf in this folder.

- **Keyboard shortcuts:** To speed up your work, look up and memorize the keyboard shortcuts for things you find yourself doing over and over. You'll find the Keyboard Commands.pdf file in the QuarkXPress 8 > Documents > English folder as well. If you're a keyboard shortcut junkie, print it out for quick reference.

Training resources

Some people prefer hands-on or visual learning, and for that you can consult the Quark Web site (www.quark.com). Click Support, then Training. You can search for a trainer or training center, watch videos, and download exercise files called QuarkEd.

Technical support

Quark provides free technical support, in English, for registered users of the latest version of QuarkXPress. Quark scatters this information about liberally, but we've collected it here so you don't have to dig for it:

- **E-mail:** If your situation falls into the "it's bugging me but not stopping my work" category, e-mail tech support and they'll generally get back to you within 24 hours. You can upload your QuarkXPress files for review as well. E-mail techsupp@quark.com or fill out the e-mail form at www.quark.com (Support > Desktop Tech Support).

- **Phone:** For those lucky emergencies that happen during the work week, call tech support at 1-800-676-4575. You can call 24 hours a day from Monday through Friday. (That's midnight on Monday morning to midnight on Friday night, Mountain Standard Time.)

If you need product information such as pricing, e-mail customer service at cservice@quark.com.

CHAPTER 1

Projects

IN MOST COMPUTER APPLICATIONS, A "FILE"—A NAMED ENTITY stored in a specific location—contains a single document. The document, whether a letter or book chapter or dining menu, is one size and usually covers one topic. Think of a picture file from a digital camera or a word processing file.

In QuarkXPress, however, a file can be more than a single document. A QuarkXPress file is called a project, not a document, and it can contain multiple documents called layouts. Layouts can be different sizes—so the same project file can contain business cards and letterhead, for example—and they can be for different media. QuarkXPress can produce print, Web, and interactive (Flash) layouts, all of which can be stored in a project file.

Storing several layouts in a project file has many advantages. For one thing, all the "supplies" for the project—such as colors, style sheets, and shared text and graphics—are available to all the layouts. Changes to shared text, for example, can be made once simultaneously for a brochure, Web site, and interactive catalog at the same time. In addition, storing layouts in projects creates fewer files to manage and back up.

In this chapter you'll learn how to save projects and create, append, delete, and export layouts.

Creating projects

A single QuarkXPress project file can contain multiple layouts for the same or different media—print, Web, and interactive (**Figure 1.1**)

FIGURE 1.1 In QuarkXPress, a project file can contain multiple layouts for the same or different media. For example, a project may contain three variations of a print layout such as a book cover in three different languages. Or, a project may contain a print, Web, and interactive version of the same content.

To create a project in QuarkXPress, you will actually create its first layout. While this is easy to do mechanically—you just click a few commands—you need to make various decisions that will affect the final output. First, you need to decide what type of layout to start the project with: print, Web, or interactive. Then, you'll need to know the finished size of the piece:

- **For print:** Figure out the finished page size after any trim. (Pages are trimmed to the final size when items such as photos bleed off the page.)

- **For Web:** Decide whether you want a fixed-page width or if you want pages that adjust according to the width of the browser window.

- For interactive: Use the height and width of the exported presentation as it will be viewed onscreen. This will vary depending on how you are distributing the presentation; for example, if it's part of a Web site, it will be smaller than if it's a full-screen presentation.

Depending on the job, you may need advice from a printer, an IT specialist, or a marketing department to make these decisions. You can, of course, change the size later, but you may end up making many time-consuming manual adjustments. Other decisions you make, such as margins, are easy to change later.

Setting up a new layout for a project

Once you know what you want to create for the first layout in the project, choose File > New > Project. Here, we will take a look at how to set up a print layout, which you are likely to do most of the time. (See Chapter 12 for how to set up Web layouts and Chapter 13 for how to set up interactive layouts.) Highlights of the New Project dialog box include:

- **Layout Name:** This is not the name of the project—it's the name of the first layout that the project will contain. While it's easy to change this later, it's a good idea to enter a descriptive name (such as Brochure) rather than leaving the default name of Layout 1.

- **Layout Type:** This is where you choose the media for the layout: Print, Web, or Interactive (**Figure 1.2**). You can change this later if necessary, but changing it will render all the other settings in this dialog box moot.

FIGURE 1.2 Use the New Project dialog box to set up the initial layout for a project.

- **Page:** The size you set up here is the *final* page size after the pages are trimmed at the printer. Do not create larger pages to contain items that bleed off the page; you can create your own bleed guides or set them up using the Guides palette (Window menu).

- **Facing Pages:** If you want to see reader spreads—the two pages you read side-by-side in a book or magazine—check Facing Pages. When this is checked, you can also set Inside and Outside margins rather than Left and Right margins for the pages.

- **Automatic Text Box:** Checking this automatically places a text box on the default master page and the first page of the layout. The automatic text box is helpful in two ways. First, you can start typing as soon as you create a new layout. Second, if you import a long text file, it automatically flows through the automatic text box, adding pages as necessary to accommodate the length of the text. This saves you the very tedious task of manually adding pages and linking boxes.

- **Margin Guides and Column Guides:** The values in the Margin Guides and Column Guides fields control the placement of default guides that you can use for item placement. They are not strict borders and are easy to change. The one important thing to know about these values is that if you use the automatic text box, it is placed snugly inside the margin guides with the number of columns specified.

When you click OK, QuarkXPress creates a new project containing the initial layout.

TIP ***PRECISION PROJECT NAMES***

Many companies have rules regarding file names—for example, the project file for a book may be named with the book's ISBN number, or an advertisement may be named with a job number. If you're working for yourself or have no rules to follow, create a file-naming strategy to ensure that files are never misplaced or confused with older versions. A common issue with project names is that they are too general. For example, if you create an ad campaign for a client and you name the project with the client's name, what do you name the second project for that client? How does the printer identify the job if they have multiple jobs for that client? And finally, if you ultimately give project files to clients, the name is useless to them—they already know their name. A good name might identify you, the client, and the job.

Saving the project

Even though you named the first layout in the New Project dialog box, the new project file is unsaved.

1. Choose File > Save or File > Save As.

2. Navigate to a location for the project file—for example, a folder for the project and client.

3. Enter a name that identifies the entire project in the Save As field—for example, the name of an advertising campaign or a magazine issue.

4. Add the file extension .qxp to the file name. While this is not required, it helps your system identify file types.

5. Leave the Type setting at the default: Project. Later, if you design a template—a pre-designed starting place for new projects—you will choose Project Template.

6. On the Mac, you can check Include Preview to see a thumbnail of the first page of the document in the Open dialog box.

TIP **SKIP THE 'DOCUMENTS' FOLDER**

When you start creating and saving projects, set up a strategy for where to save them—a folder for each client with subfolders for each job, for example. In general, you will want to store all the content for a project (text files, picture files, and so on) in a single folder. Saving projects in the Windows My Documents folder, or just whatever location opens in the Save As dialog box, quickly leads to confusion about where files are.

TIP **DEFAULT PATH FOR SAVE AS**

If you tend to save files in the same location, you can have QuarkXPress automatically open the Save As dialog box to that location. In the Preferences dialog box, click Default Path at left and check Use Default Path for Save/Save As. Use the Browse button to navigate to your preferred location.

Working in single-layout mode

All QuarkXPress projects contain at least one layout, so all projects involve at least two names. You have the name of the project file and the name of the layout. In many cases, projects simply contain one layout—an ad, a sticker design, a brochure—and having two names is pointless.

If you prefer a single name for the layout and project, check Single Layout Mode in the New Project dialog box. The Layout Name field disappears and you name the project in the Save As dialog box. If you rarely or never store multiple layouts in the same project file, check Single Layout Mode in the Project > General pane of the Preferences dialog box (**Figure 1.3**). You will never be bothered with layout and project names again.

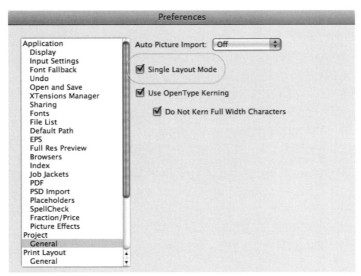

FIGURE 1.3 The Single Layout Mode preference simplifies project and layout naming when most of your project files contain only one layout.

TIP **SINGLE-LAYOUT MODE FOR LOOKS ONLY**

Veteran users will appreciate working in single-layout mode because it sends QuarkXPress back in time to versions 1 through 5. But even if you prefer to work this way most of the time, single-layout mode is nonrestrictive. You can still add and duplicate layouts as you wish.

Opening projects

You open QuarkXPress project files the same way you open any file on your system: Choose File > Open, double-click the filename on your desktop, or drag the file on top of the application icon. The project opens to the last layout you were editing. A few things may happen when you open a project:

- **Nonmatching Preferences alert:** If a long, complicated alert displays regarding preferences, click Keep Document Settings. This ensures that nothing changes in the layouts within the project file.

- **Missing Fonts alert:** If any layout in the project uses fonts that are not active on your system, click List Fonts. Note the missing fonts and activate them through a font manager or through your system. You can also replace the missing fonts with active fonts, but this can change the design of the layouts.

- **Modified Pictures alert:** If an alert indicates that pictures files imported into one of the layouts have been modified, click List Pictures to see which ones. (This might happen if you import a picture file into a layout, then perform more edits to the picture or graphic in Adobe Photoshop or Adobe Illustrator.) You can then update the pictures, which updates the previews displayed in QuarkXPress and the links to the files. This alert only displays when the Auto Picture Import preference for the project is set to Verify (Preferences > Project > General).

If you need to take a quick look at a file, it's fine to bypass the Missing Fonts and Modified Pictures alerts. For final output, however, it's important that the correct fonts are active and all picture files are updated.

TIP ***USE A FONT MANAGEMENT PROGRAM***

For most graphic designers, the font management tools available through your system are not adequate for managing the volume and variety of fonts you eventually have. A professional font manager such as Suitcase Fusion (www.extensis.com) provides expert features for locating specific fonts, previewing them, and controlling which specific fonts are active. Some font managers also provide QuarkXPress XTensions (plug-in software modules) that activate fonts automatically as projects are opened.

Creating layouts

Projects can contain an unlimited number of layouts. Once in a project, layouts can be shared and exported—they are not stuck within the project file. Nonetheless, you will not want to get too crazy storing layouts within projects. You want to keep the project file at a reasonable size so you can burn it on a DVD to share or archive, for example. To create a new layout within the active project:

1. Choose Layout > New. Or, to create a copy of the active layout, choose Layout > Duplicate.

2. In the Layout Properties dialog box (**Figure 1.4**), enter a Layout Name and choose a Layout Type.

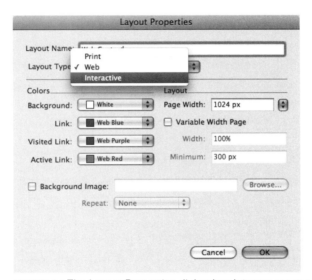

FIGURE 1.4 The Layout Properties dialog box lets you name and configure new layouts.

3. Use the remaining controls to configure the print, Web, or interactive layout.

When you click OK, the new layout displays.

To control which layout displays, click the tabs at the top of the project window (Figure 1.5).

FIGURE 1.5 Tabs at the top of the project window let you control which layout displays. Here, the project contains a print brochure, Web page, and interactive Flash file of the same content.

TIP **CHANGE LAYOUT PROPERTIES**

You can change any characteristic of a layout, including its name, type, and size. For example, you might duplicate a print layout and then change its type to a Web layout to get started on a Web page. To do this, choose Layout > Properties. Changing layout properties may alter the content—for example, if you change a Web layout that contains interactive elements to a print layout, the interactivity will be lost. A warning displays if the layout's contents may change.

Appending layouts

Millions of files exist in QuarkXPress format. If you happen to have or inherit some of those pre-existing files, most are in the old one-document-per-file format. To take advantage of the benefits of storing multiple layouts in a project file—such as shared style sheets and master pages—you can import layouts from existing QuarkXPress files into project files. To append a layout into the active project:

1. Choose File > Append.

2. Navigate to and select the document (from QuarkXPress 3.3–5.x) or project (from QuarkXPress 6 and above). The Append dialog box may take a few seconds to open, depending on how old the document is or how many layouts the project contains.

3. In the Append list at left, click Layout.

4. In the Available list in the center, click the layouts you want to append. Click the right-facing arrow to send the layouts over to the Including list (**Figure** 1.6).

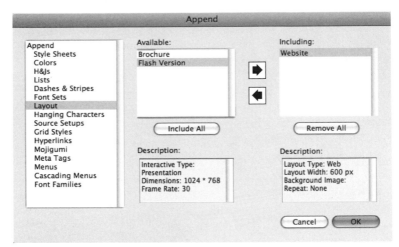

FIGURE 1.6 Use the Append dialog box to import layouts from QuarkXPress 3.3–5.x documents and from QuarkXPress 6.0 and above projects.

5. When you click OK, an alert warns you that style sheets, colors, master pages, and so on are going to come along with this layout. You can click OK again—if necessary, you will be able to resolve conflicts such as colors with the same name but different definitions.

Once you append a layout, save the project file.

TIP **RESOLVING CONFLICTS**

If the Append Conflict dialog box displays, you can carefully review conflicting definitions such as differences in H&Js or color definitions. This can be tedious and difficult, so it may be better to click Auto-Rename and then check Repeat for All Conflicts. This places an asterisk in front of the imported style sheet, color, H&J, or whatever. You can then review the usage in the layout and decide whether to keep the old settings or use the settings in the project. For example, say a project contains a style sheet called Body that specifies Adobe Garamond Pro and you append a layout with a style sheet called Body that specifies ITC Garamond. Text will probably reflow significantly if you override the appended layout's style sheet with the project's style sheet. If you rename the Body style sheet in the appended layout, you can review the layout to see if you want to change the style sheet or not.

Exporting and deleting layouts

Not only can you import layouts through File > Append, but you can export layouts through File > Export. You can export one layout as a separate project file or select several layouts to store in a new project file. You might export a layout in order to share a template or a smaller file with another user, for example. (You do not need to export a layout to send only that layout to a printer—use File > Collect for Output to do that.) When you no longer need a layout in a project, you can delete it.

Exporting layouts

To export a layout from the active project:

Choose File > Export > Layouts as Project.

In the Export Layouts as Project dialog box (**Figure 1.7**), specify a name and location for the new project that will contain the exported layouts.

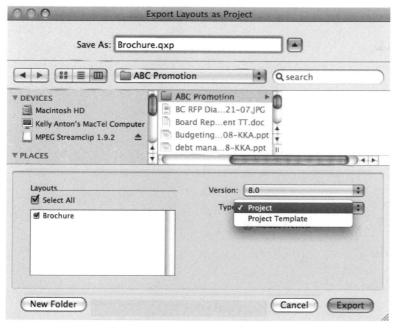

FIGURE 1.7 The Export Layouts as Project dialog box lets you extract selected layouts as separate projects and downsave layouts for use in QuarkXPress 7.

3. In the Layouts area in the lower-left corner, make sure only the layouts you want to export are checked.

4. If you are exporting a layout to serve as a template, choose Project Template from the Type menu. Templates, which serve as a pre-designed starting place a new layout, are write-protected files that open as new, unsaved projects.

Exported layouts are copied into new projects, so they remain in the source project. After exporting a layout, you may want to delete it from the source project.

TIP **DOWNSAVING TO QUARKXPRESS 7**

If you need to open a QuarkXPress 8 layout in QuarkXPress 7, you have to export the layout from the project—even if it's the only layout in the project. In the Export Layouts as Project dialog box, choose 7.0 from the Version menu. Be sure to change the file name or location so you can easily distinguish the 7.0 version from the 8.0 version.

Deleting layouts

If you no longer want a layout in a project—because you exported it, because that part of the job was canceled, or whatever—you can delete it. If you want to save any of the content, you can export a layout before you delete it or save some of the contents in a library (see Chapter 4). To delete the active layout, choose Layout > Delete. When the alert displays a warning that this cannot be undone, click OK.

CHAPTER 2

Workspace

The QuarkXPress 8 default workspace is designed to put all the tools and controls you need right at your fingertips. With easy access to design options, you can let your creativity flow as you compose layouts, fine-tune text, and manipulate images onscreen. QuarkXPress tools make it easy to create and modify items, the palettes provide a convenient path to formatting controls, and layout aids such as rulers and guides help with placement.

You can customize the workspace by displaying the palettes and layout aids you need, saving palette sets, resizing and splitting project windows, and more. As you work in QuarkXPress, you'll need to navigate through layouts and pages, change the view scale, and experiment with items on the pasteboard surrounding layout pages. Since nothing can stymie your creative inspiration more than having to hunt through the program interface for a command you need, familiarize yourself with the QuarkXPress workspace in these pages.

In this chapter you'll learn about the QuarkXPress interface, including the main project window, the primary palettes, navigation and viewing options, and other interface-related features.

Project windows

The main project window displays all the palettes you have open, the layouts within the project, and the pages of the selected layout (**Figure 2.1**).

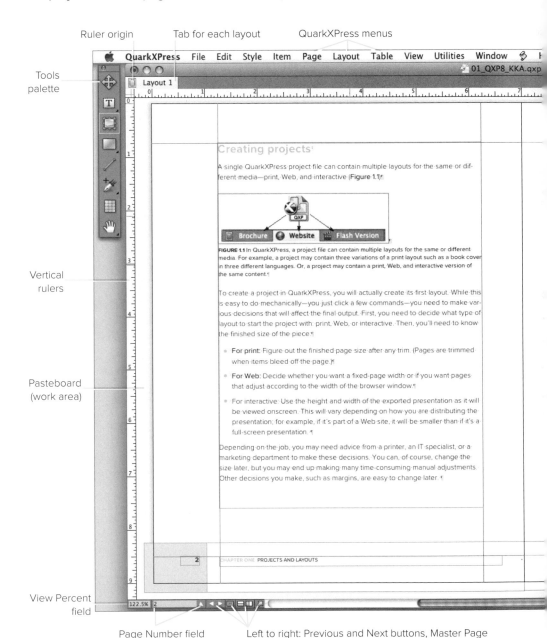

Ruler origin

Tab for each layout

QuarkXPress menus

Tools palette

Vertical rulers

Pasteboard (work area)

View Percent field

Page Number field and Thumbnails menu

Left to right: Previous and Next buttons, Master Page toggle, Split Window buttons, and Export menu

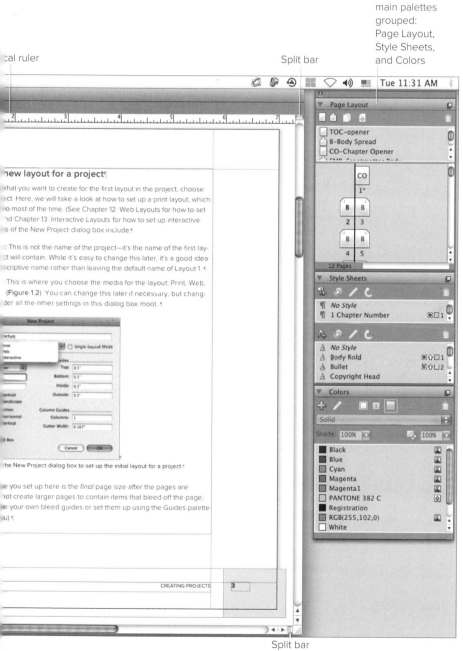

Three of the
main palettes
grouped:
Page Layout,
Style Sheets,
and Colors

cal ruler

Split bar

Tue 11:31 AM

▼ Page Layout

TOC-opener
B-Body Spread
CO-Chapter Opener

CO
1*

B   B
2   3

B   B
4   5

12 Pages

▼ Style Sheets

¶ *No Style*
¶ 1 Chapter Number   ⌘□1

A *No Style*
A Body Bold   ⌘⇧□1
A Bullet   ⌘⇧□2
A Copyright Head

▼ Colors

Solid

Shade: 100%   100%

■ Black
■ Blue
□ Cyan
■ Magenta
■ Magenta1
□ PANTONE 382 C
■ Registration
□ RGB(255,102,0)
□ White

new layout for a project¶

what you want to create for the first layout in the project, choose
ect. Here, we will take a look at how to set up a print layout, which
o most of the time. (See Chapter 12 Web Layouts for how to set
nd Chapter 13 Interactive Layouts for how to set up interactive
s of the New Project dialog box include¶

: This is not the name of the project—it's the name of the first lay-
ct will contain. While it's easy to change this later, it's a good idea
scriptive name rather than leaving the default name of Layout 1.¶

This is where you choose the media for the layout: Print, Web,
(Figure 1.2). You can change this later if necessary, but chang-
der all the other settings in this dialog box moot. ¶

New Project

the New Project dialog box to set up the initial layout for a project.¶

e you set up here is the *final* page size after the pages are
not create larger pages to contain items that bleed off the page;
e your own bleed guides or set them up using the Guides palette
u).¶

CREATING PROJECTS   3

Split bar

FIGURE 2.1: The QuarkXPress project window.

Splitting project windows

QuarkXPress lets you split the project window to see different views of projects within the layout. For example, while you're working, you might want to see how adjusting the runaround on a picture affects all the text in a box, or you might need to see if adding text in one location causes reflow across a layout (**Figure 2.2**).

To split the project window horizontally or vertically, click the split-screen icons on the lower-left corner of the project window ▤▥ or choose Window > Split Window > Horizontal (or Vertical). You can also drag the small, light blue split bar ▚ in the lower-right corner of the project window for a vertical split or the upper-right corner for a horizontal split. The size of the original window determines how many times it can be split. Drag the split bar between windows to adjust the window sizes.

To remove a split, click a window's close box or drag the split bar to any side of the project window. You can also choose Window > Split Window > Remove All.

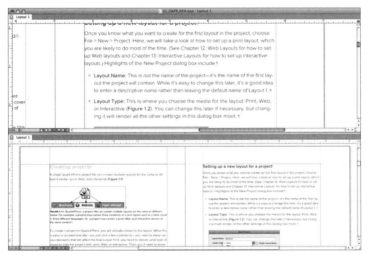

FIGURE 2.2: Splitting the project window allows you to display different views of the same layout or display a different layout.

Opening new project windows

To open a new window for the active project, choose Window > New Window. You can drag the new window to another monitor, view different layouts in that window, and more. This is particularly helpful if you are updating shared content among layouts. To close a separate window, click its close box.

Tools palette

The Tools palette provides all the tools you need for creating, selecting, and modifying QuarkXPress items and their contents. You will generally keep the Tools palette open at all times, but you can open and close it quickly by pressing F8 or choosing Window > Tools. Select tools with the mouse or with keyboard shortcuts.

Reviewing the tools

A small triangle in the lower-right corner of a tool's box indicates a pop-out menu of additional tools. The default Tools palette provides the tools shown in **Figure 2.3**; the tools in the pop-outs are shown in **Figures 2.4–2.7**.

Select the Item tool to work with items (boxes, lines, tables, groups), including moving, resizing, and formatting.

Select the Text Content tool to edit text in boxes, on lines, and in table cells; you can also create text boxes.

Select the Picture Content tool to modify pictures; you can also draw picture boxes.

Select the Rectangle Box tool to create boxes (for text, pictures, and more); press Shift to create square boxes.

Select the Line tool to create straight lines at any angle; press Shift to create horizontal or vertical lines.

Select the Bézier Pen tool to create curved lines and boxes; press Shift to constrain lines to 45 degrees.

Select the Table tool to draw a new table; a dialog box displays so you can specify the number of rows and columns.

Select the Zoom tool to increase the layout's view scale; press Option/Alt to decrease the view scale.

FIGURE 2.3: The default Tools palette.

To select a tool in a pop-out menu, click the main tool, then drag to the right. The tool replaces the initial tool. Press Control as you select a tool to add it to the Tools palette. To move the tool back to its pop-out menu, Control+click it.

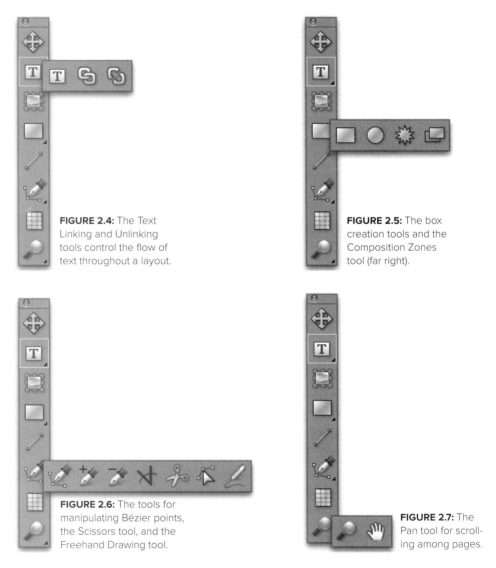

FIGURE 2.4: The Text Linking and Unlinking tools control the flow of text throughout a layout.

FIGURE 2.5: The box creation tools and the Composition Zones tool (far right).

FIGURE 2.6: The tools for manipulating Bézier points, the Scissors tool, and the Freehand Drawing tool.

FIGURE 2.7: The Pan tool for scrolling among pages.

TIP **DISPLAYING TOOLS HORIZONTALLY ON WINDOWS**

On Windows, you can display the Tools palette horizontally by pressing Control as you double-click the palette's title bar.

Selecting tools with keyboard shortcuts

Single-letter keyboard shortcuts let you quickly change tools. (If you're using the Text Content tool, press Escape first.) When different tools have the same shortcut, press the shortcut key repeatedly until the tool you want is selected.

You can also gain "temporary access" to some tools by pressing a keyboard shortcut. For example, while editing text with the Text Content tool, you can press Command (Mac) Control (Windows) for the Item tool and move the box. When you release the key, the previous tool is still selected.

- **Item tool:** V or Command (Mac) or Control (Windows) for temporary access.

- **Text Content tool, Text Linking tool, Text Unlinking tool:** T or double-click a box with the Item tool for the Text Content tool.

- **Picture Content tool:** R or double-click a picture with the Item tool.

- **Rectangle Box tool, Oval Box tool, Star Box tool, Composition Zones tool:** B.

- **Line tool:** L.

- **Bézier Pen tool, Add Point tool, Remove Point tool, Convert Point tool, Scissors tool, Select Point tool, Freehand Drawing tool:** P.

- **Table tool:** G.

- **Zoom tool:** Z or Control+Shift (Mac)/Control+spacebar (Windows) for temporary access.

- **Pan tool:** X or Option (Mac)/Alt (Windows) for temporary access.

Menus and context menus

Even QuarkXPress beginners will have no trouble using the QuarkXPress menus. You may wish to click each menu to see how commands are grouped. Just don't get bewildered by the sheer length and complexity of the commands—many of the menu commands are special-purpose options that you'll never touch.

A few notes about the QuarkXPress menus:

- **Preferences dialog box:** The Mac version provides a QuarkXPress menu, where you will find the Preferences command. (On Windows, you'll find Preferences under the Edit menu.)

- **Context-sensitive menus:** The options in the Style menu (**Figure 2.8**) change entirely depending on whether text, a picture, or a line is selected in the layout. In other menus, commands are grayed out if they are not relevant to the layout type (print, Web, or interactive) or the selected item.

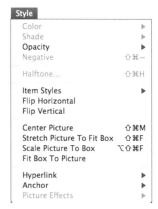

FIGURE 2.8: The Style menu for pictures displays when a picture is selected.

- **Context menus:** You can make quick changes to everything from the rulers to the project window to the selected item with context menus (**Figure 2.9**). Control+click/right+click anywhere on the window or page to see the options.

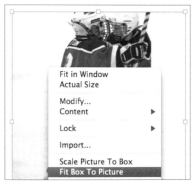

FIGURE 2.9: The context menu for a picture lets you lock it, scale it, and more.

Measurements palette

The Measurements palette puts scores of formatting controls for text, pictures, and items front and center. The palette is divided into tabs of related controls along with a Classic tab that consolidates the most frequently used options for formatting both items and contents (Figure 2.10). As with the Tools palette, you will generally keep the Measurements palette open at all times. You can open and close it quickly by pressing F9 or choosing Window > Measurements.

FIGURE 2.10: The Classic tab of the Measurements palette combines the most-often used formatting controls, with item formatting options on the left and content formatting options on the right. When text is selected, as shown above, the left side lets you change the placement, size, and color of the box itself. The right side provides formatting options such as alignment and font.

Reviewing Measurements palette options

The availability of the tabs in the Measurements palette depends on what is selected in the layout—text, a picture, an item, a group, a table, and so on—and what type of layout you're working on. Tabs include Classic, Text, Paragraph, Character, Tabs, Frame, Runaround, Clipping, Text Path, Space/Align, Export, Grids, and Drop Shadow. Figures 2.11–2.13 show a variety of basic Measurement palette tabs.

FIGURE 2.11: When a picture is selected, the Classic tab of the Measurements palette provides box controls (such as size) at left and picture controls (such as scale) at right.

FIGURE 2.12: When a text box is selected, the Text tab of the Measurements palette lets you control the placement of text within the box, including the number of columns and text inset.

FIGURE 2.13: The Drop Shadow tab of the Measurements palette provides the controls for applying a drop shadow to whatever is selected—text, a picture, or an item.

Displaying Measurements palette tabs

By default, the Classic tab of the Measurements palette displays tabs for the current selection. To select another tab, hover the mouse above the Measurements palette to display the tab bar and select a button. Since you will use the various tabs of the Measurements palette often, you can set the tab bar to always display. To do this, Control+click/right-click the Measurements palette title bar (on the far left side) and choose Always Show Tab Bar (**Figure 2.14**).

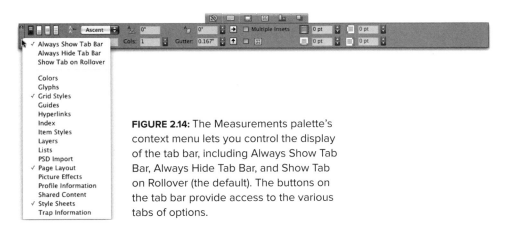

FIGURE 2.14: The Measurements palette's context menu lets you control the display of the tab bar, including Always Show Tab Bar, Always Hide Tab Bar, and Show Tab on Rollover (the default). The buttons on the tab bar provide access to the various tabs of options.

Calculating measurements in fields

When you enter values in fields in the Measurements palette—or fields in any dialog box—you can enter math operators so QuarkXPress can calculate values for you. For example, to cut the width of a 3.12" box in half, you can enter /2 next to the value in the Width field. To double the width of the box, you can enter *2. The math operators are: + (plus), − (minus), * (multiply), / (divide).

Palette management

The palettes in QuarkXPress are both a blessing and a curse. They make frequently used controls readily available while cluttering your screen and obscuring your layouts. Having a second monitor for storing palettes is handy, but it does put them a little out of reach. To get control of palettes and keep them close by, you can open, close, and resize them; group them; and save palette configurations as sets to show and hide together.

Palette overview

Palettes are small floating windows that condense a lot of related features into a little space. All the QuarkXPress palettes are listed in the Window menu. In general, you will have at least the Tools palette and the Measurements palette open, along with possibly the Page Layout, Colors, and Style Sheets palettes. Palettes work as follows:

Open: Choose a palette name from the Window menu to open it.

Close: Click the close button in the upper-left corner or choose a palette name from the Window menu to close it.

Resize: Drag the lower-left corner of the palette to resize it. (Some palettes are a fixed size.) Click the arrow next to the palette's name to shrink the palette to just its title bar.

Palette menus: Click the menu icon in the upper-right corner of a palette's title bar to display a menu of options specific to the palette (**Figure 2.15**).

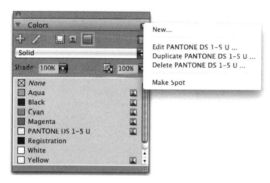

FIGURE 2.15: Palette menus let you edit the contents of a palette and perform related tasks. For example, the Colors palette menu lets you create, edit, duplicate, and delete colors and convert the selected color from Spot to Process and vice versa.

Creating palette groups

QuarkXPress lets you group palettes vertically so they travel together. To group palettes, Control+click (Mac) or right+click (Windows) the title bar of any palette (**Figure 2.16**). From the context menu, choose a palette to add it to the current palette or group. You can also detach palettes from a group and close palettes from this context menu.

FIGURE 2.16: Control+click/right+click a palette's title bar to make changes to the palette's group.

Saving palette sets

Once you create a palette configuration that you like—including which palettes are open, how they are grouped, and where they are—you can save the configuration as a palette set. You can create multiple palette sets for different purposes, such as editing text or working with color and pictures. To create a palette set, first set up your palettes the way you want them. Then, choose Window > Palette Sets > Save Palette Set As. Give the palette set a descriptive name and specify a keyboard shortcut for it if you want (**Figure 2.17**). To display a palette set, choose it from the Window > Palette Sets submenu or press its keyboard shortcut.

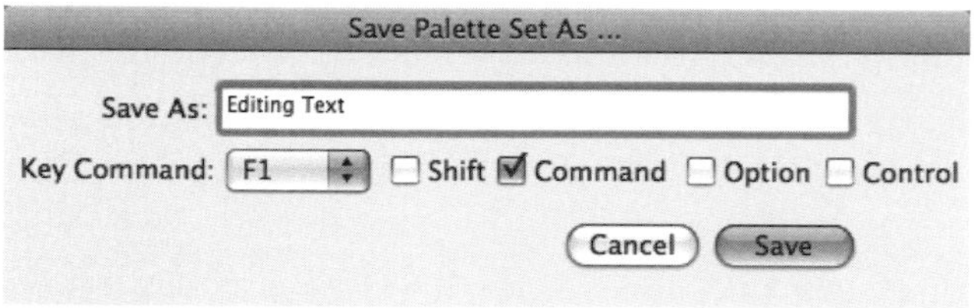

FIGURE 2.17: Palette sets save a palette configuration, including the open palettes, the palette groups, and their locations.

Navigation

When you're designing and revising a layout, it can seem like you're spending half your time just locating the right spot to work on. QuarkXPress provides many ways to navigate through layouts, including "turning" pages and entering page numbers as well as more visual methods such as clicking page icons. Most users find a navigation method they like best and stick with it.

- **Scroll bars:** Using the scroll bars is probably the slowest and least accurate way to navigate in QuarkXPress. Nonetheless, as in all programs, you can scroll within pages and from page to page.

- **Pan tool:** The Pan tool lets you "push" pages around until you get to just the right spot. Similar to scrolling, panning can be somewhat slow, but it's very visual and can give you a good overview of a layout. The Pan tool is in a pop-out menu of the Zoom tool at the bottom of the Tools palette. You can select it from the pop-out or press X. (You may need to press X twice as X is also assigned to the Zoom tool; X will not select the Pan tool when the Text Content tool is selected.) A better way to access the Pan tool is by holding down Option (Mac) or Alt (Windows). Rather than selecting the Pan tool, this just gives you temporary access to it so you can move around the layout, then go back to what you were doing with the previously selected tool.

- **Turn pages:** To flip from page to page, you can use the arrows in the lower-left corner of the project window , the Page Up and Page Down keys on your keyboard, or the options in the Page menu: Previous, Next, First, and Last. Pressing Page Up and Page Down on the keyboard moves up or down an entire spread. Add the Shift key to move up or down one page; add the Option (Mac) or Alt (Windows) key to view the same area of the previous or next page.

- **Select page icons:** You can double-click a page icon in the Page Layout palette (Window menu) to jump to that page. In addition, if you click the up arrow `30%` `35` `▲◄►` next to the Page Number field in the lower-left corner of the project window, you can choose from a menu of page icons.

- **Enter page numbers:** If you know what page you want to display, you can enter its number in the Page Number field in the lower-left corner of the project window `35` `▲◄►`. The quickest way to jump to a page—without taking your hands off the keyboard—is to use the keyboard shortcut for the Page > Go To menu command. Press Command+J (Mac) or Control+J (Windows), enter a number, and press Return/Enter.

TIP *ENTERING PAGE NUMBERS*

When you enter page numbers, you need to include any section numbering. So if the page number shows 1.2, you need to enter 1.2. If you don't know the section number, you can enter an "absolute" page number according to the page's position in the layout. To enter an absolute page number, precede it with a plus sign—so +1 is the first page in the layout, +2 is the second, and so on. You can also quickly jump to the last page of a layout by entering the word "end." This information applies to page numbers you enter in any fields—for navigation, printing, moving pages, and the like.

Layout aids

QuarkXPress provides a variety of visual aids that help with sizing and positioning items on pages. You can customize many of these aids in preferences and control which ones are showing. You might show all the layout aids while constructing a layout, then hide them all for fine-tuning.

TIP *MEMORIZE KEYBOARD SHORTCUTS FOR FAVORITES*

Memorize the keyboard shortcuts for showing and hiding the rulers—Command+R (Mac) or Control+R (Windows)—as you may show and hide them often. If you tend to use grids, notice the keyboard shortcuts listed in the menu and memorize the ones you use.

Viewing layout aids

Choose options from the View menu (**Figure 2.18**) to control which layout aids display, including:

- **Guides:** Choose View > Guides to display margin guides, ruler guides, and any guides you created through the Guides palette (Window menu).

- **Page grids:** Choose View > Page Grids to display each page's grid.

- **Text box grids:** Choose View > Text Box Grids to display any grids applied to text boxes in the layout.

- **Rulers and ruler direction:** Choose View > Rulers to display a horizontal ruler across the top of the project window along with a vertical ruler down the left side. By default, the ruler measures pages from left to right. The View > Ruler Direction submenu lets you choose Left-to-Right or Right-to-Left.

- **Invisibles:** Choose View > Invisibles to display nonprinting characters in text such as spaces (dots), tabs (arrows), and paragraph returns (¶). Invisibles are particularly helpful when creating tabs and applying style sheets.

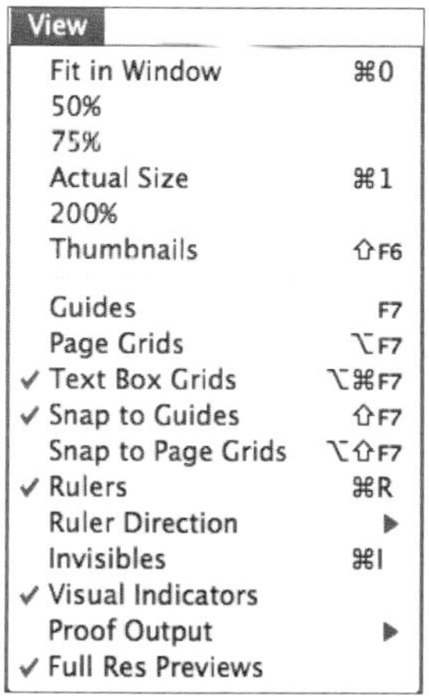

View	
Fit in Window	⌘0
50%	
75%	
Actual Size	⌘1
200%	
Thumbnails	⇧F6
Guides	F7
Page Grids	⌥F7
✓ Text Box Grids	⌥⌘F7
✓ Snap to Guides	⇧F7
Snap to Page Grids	⌥⇧F7
✓ Rulers	⌘R
Ruler Direction	▶
Invisibles	⌘I
✓ Visual Indicators	
Proof Output	▶
✓ Full Res Previews	

FIGURE 2.18: In the bottom portion of the View menu, the checked options display onscreen.

Snapping to guides

You can also activate the Snap to Guides and Snap to Page Grids commands in the View menu. When checked, these options create a sort of "magnetic field" around guides so that items automatically align with them. The size of the magnetic field, called the Snap Distance, is specified in the Guides & Grids pane of the Preferences dialog box.

Customizing layout aids

You can customize most of the layout aids in QuarkXPress—for example, you can change the default color of guides if they are the same color as a layout's background. Or, you can work in picas or centimeters instead of inches. To customize the layout aids:

- **Guides:** Specify the color of margin guides and ruler guides in the Grids & Guides pane of the Preferences dialog box. The Guides palette (Window menu) lets you specify the color of individual guides as well.

- **Page Grids:** Specify the color of gridlines in the Master Guides & Grids dialog box when a master page is displayed.

- **Text Box Grids:** Specify the color of gridlines through the Grid Settings dialog box (context menu > Grid Settings) or a grid style (Window > Grid Styles).

- **Rulers:** The Measurements pane of the Preferences dialog box lets you choose from Inches, Inches Decimal, Picas, Points, Millimeters, Centimeters, Ciceros, and Agates for the horizontal and vertical rulers. You can also Control+click (Mac) or right+click (Windows) the rulers and choose an option from the Measure submenu of the context menu.

TIP ***CHANGING THE MEASUREMENT SYSTEM***

The measurement system selected for the rulers affects all the measurement fields in the software (Origin Across, Origin Down, Width, Height, and so on). If you want to enter a value in a different measurement system—for example, if you want to enter a value in inches while the measurement system is set to picas—enter the measurement system's standard abbreviation (such as " or cm) with the value. QuarkXPress will convert the values for you. Note that font size, line width, and frame width are always specified in points, regardless of the selected measurement system.

View options

QuarkXPress lets you view layouts at anywhere from 10% to 800% of their actual size—so you can, for example, zoom out to get a quick overview of an entire publication or zoom in to carefully position a single letter or box. Since you change the view scale often as you work, QuarkXPress provides a variety of convenient methods for changing the view. In addition, you can view imported pictures at their full resolution to see all the details.

Changing the view scale

You can change the view scale by using the Zoom tool, choosing commands in the View menu, and entering a value in the View Percent field on the project window. If you have a split window, you can view the same layout at different view percentages, allowing you to see the effect of detailed changes on an entire layout.

Zoom tool: Use the Zoom tool at the bottom of the Tools palette to increase the layout view scale; press Option (Mac) or Alt (Windows) to decrease the view scale. You can click the Zoom tool to change the view in standard increments or you can click and drag to view a specific area of a layout. Press V (when you're not using the Text Content tool) to select the Zoom tool. You can also press Control+Shift (Mac) or Control+spacebar (Windows) for temporary access to the Zoom tool.

Keyboard commands: Press Command (Mac) or Control (Windows) along with the plus (+) or minus (-) sign on the keyboard to change the view in standard increments. When using the Text Content tool, press Escape first.

View menu: Choose an option from the View menu to change the view scale: Fit in Window, 50%, 75%, Actual Size, 200%, and Thumbnails. You are likely to use Fit in Window and Actual Size (100%) often enough that you should remember those shortcuts: Command+zero (Mac) or Control+zero (Windows) for Fit in Window; change the zero to 1 for 100%. Thumbnails view (around 10%) lets you move pages within a layout and drag pages among projects.

Enter a percent value. Enter a specific value in the View Percent field in the lower-left corner of the project window . You can quickly jump to this field by pressing Control+V (Mac) or Control+Alt+V (Windows), entering a value, and pressing Return/Enter. Enter "t" for Thumbnails view.

Viewing full-resolution previews

If the files for imported pictures are available on your computer, you can enable full-resolution previews for individual pictures. Full-resolution picture previews are smooth (not pixelated) and give you a better idea of how the final output will look. To enable a full-resolution preview, select the picture and choose Item > Preview Resolution > Full Resolution. To enable and disable the display of full-resolution previews for those pictures, choose View > Full Res Previews.

Pasteboard

Every page or spread of a QuarkXPress layout is surrounded by a work area called the pasteboard (**Figure 2.19**). You can use the pasteboard for temporary item storage and to work on items without distractions. For example, if you're drawing a new logo with the Bézier Pen tool, you might want to work on the pasteboard so you can really focus on the drawing. You can then drag the finished item to a layout page. To see the pasteboard, reduce the view scale or scroll.

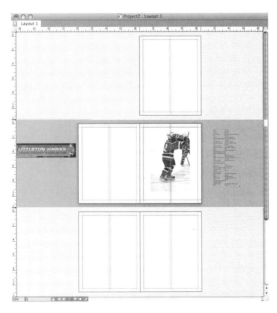

FIGURE 2.19: QuarkXPress provides a wide pasteboard to the left and right of each page or spread. Use the pasteboard for item storage, workspace, and bleed items as you work. You can specify that the pasteboard for the active spread display in a different color as shown here.

You can customize the width and color of the pasteboard, and you can specify a different color for the pasteboard of the active spread. The default pasteboard width is 100%, meaning that the pasteboard is the same width as the layout pages. You can make the pasteboard narrower but not wider. The Display pane of the Preferences dialog box (**Figure 2.20**) lets you customize the pasteboard. Display preferences are not project- or layout-specific; they apply to your copy of QuarkXPress.

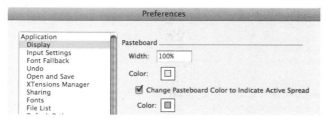

FIGURE 2.20: The Pasteboard area in the Display pane of the Preferences dialog box lets you change the default pasteboard width and color as well as specify a color to indicate the active spread.

TIP **THE PASTEBOARD AND BLEEDS**

To create bleeds—items that print beyond trimmed page edges—items on layout pages extend onto the pasteboard.

Program language

You can display the QuarkXPress 8 interface—including menu commands and palette controls—in many different languages. To do this, choose an option from the Edit > Program Language submenu (**Figure 2.21**). If you need to reset the language to U.S. English (or your preferred language) and cannot read the commands, click the Edit menu. (The Edit menu will be the second or third menu from the left, depending on your operating system.) Notice the gray dividing lines in the menu; display the second submenu under the fourth line. If you can't figure out which command is U.S. English (for example, if you don't recognize the word "Inglés"), experiment with the different options.

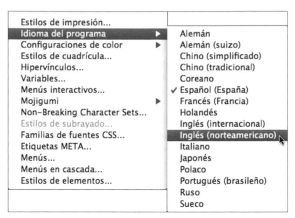

FIGURE 2.21: Here, the interface is displayed in Español; choosing Inglés (norteamericano) changes the interface language to U.S. English.

NOTE *LANGUAGE CHARACTER ATTRIBUTE*

The Program Language is not related to the Language character attribute, which is assigned through the Character Attributes dialog box (Style menu). The Language character attribute is used for spell check and hyphenation.

CHAPTER 3

Items

IF YOU DECONSTRUCT ANY PRINT PUBLICATION into its basic components, even the most complex ones boil down to text, photos, illustrations, and graphic embellishments such as lines and shapes. Each time you create a new QuarkXPress print project, you begin with a blank page and then build the publication by adding text and graphic elements to the page and, if you're creating a multipage publication, by adding more pages, each of which has its own text and graphic elements.

In this chapter you'll learn how to create several kinds of page elements—collectively referred to as items in QuarkXPress. These items are the building blocks of all the publications you'll create. You'll also learn how to manipulate the items you make by moving and resizing them and by modifying their appearance, and you'll learn how to use several features that help you work efficiently with these items.

QuarkXPress has several tools that let you create different types of items. Here's a list of the item-creation tools and what they produce:

- The Text Content tool ⊞ lets you make rectangular boxes that hold text.

- The Picture Content tool ▣ lets you create rectangular boxes that hold imported graphics.

- The Rectangle ▢, Oval ◯, and Starburst ✺ tools (which are grouped together in the Tools palette) let you create no-content boxes, which are empty shapes that don't initially contain anything. You can choose File > Import to place a picture or text into a no-content box, which changes it to a picture box or a text box. You can also double-click a no-content box with the Text Content tool to convert it to a text box. No-content boxes can be used as graphic elements by applying a background color or blend, a frame, or a special effect like a drop shadow.

- The Line tool ╱ lets you draw straight lines.

- The Bézier Pen ✎ and Freehand Drawing ✎ tools (also grouped together in the Tools palette) let you create complex lines and no-content boxes.

- The Table tool ▦ lets you make a rectangular box that contains a table.

- Type paths (Figure 3.1) are straight or curved lines created with the Line, Bézier Pen, or Freehand Drawing tools along which text flows. (To create a text path, you must first draw a line and then double-click the line with the Text Content tool.)

FIGURE 3.1 A type path is a straight or curved line along which text flows. In this example, the Bézier Pen tool was used to create the curved line. Double-clicking the line with the Text Content tool converted the line into a type path.

Creating an item using any of the item-creation tools—with the exception of the Bézier Pen and Freehand Drawing tools—is a two-step process. (You'll learn how to use the two drawing tools a little later in this chapter.)

1. Click once on the tool that will produce the kind of item you want to add to your publication. For example, if you need a rectangular text box, select the Text Content tool. If the tool you need is grouped with other tools, you may have to select it from a pop-up list. When you select an item-creation tool, the crosshairs pointer is displayed.

2. Move the crosshairs pointer to the area of the page or pasteboard where you want to place the item, and then click and drag in any direction to build a rectangle. As you drag, a rectangle is displayed (**Figure 3.2**). Release the mouse when the rectangle is approximately the size of the item you want.

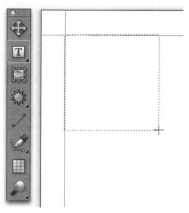

FIGURE 3.2 In this example, the Text Content tool was used to create a text box.

> **TIP: CREATING SQUARES AND CIRCLES**
>
> *If you hold down the Shift key when you click and drag to create an item, you'll create a perfect square or circle instead of a rectangle or an oval (depending on the tool you're using).*

After you create an item, it is selected. That is, it's displayed with resizing handles that you can drag to resize the item. At this point, you can continue clicking and dragging to create new items, or you can switch tools and move on to another task, such as modifying the item you just created. If you've created a text box, the flashing cursor indicates that you can begin typing to place text in the box, or you can choose File > Import to import text from a text file. (For more information about importing text, see Chapter 4.) If you've created a picture box, you can choose

File > Import to place a picture into the box. (For more information about importing pictures, see Chapter 7.)

TIP: **CREATING NONRECTANGULAR TEXT AND PICTURE BOXES**

*If you want to place text or a picture within a nonrectangular shape (**Figure 3.3**), first use any of the drawing tools that let you create nonrectangular no-content boxes (for example, the Oval Box tool or the Bézier Pen tool). With the item selected, choose Item > Content, and then choose Text or Picture from the submenu.*

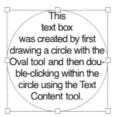

FIGURE 3.3 Any closed shape can be used as a text box.

TIP: **CREATING REGULAR POLYGONS**

Oddly, there's no easy way to create regular polygons (triangles, pentagons, hexagons, and so on, with equal angles and equal sides) in QuarkXPress, but there's a relatively simple workaround. Use the Starburst tool to create a shape that has twice as many spikes as the number of sides you want for your polygon. (Double-click the Starburst Tool to configure it.) Hold down the Shift key as you drag to create a starburst shape so that all sides and all angles are equal. Select the Delete Point tool (it's grouped with the Bézier Pen tool in the Tools panel), and then delete every other point.

Using the drawing tools

The Freehand Drawing tool [icon] and the Bézier Pen tool [icon] let you create freeform lines and shapes and open up all sorts of creative possibilities; however, using these tools—particularly the Bézier Pen—is a little trickier than using the other item-creation tools. Don't worry if you don't feel comfortable right away. The more you use these tools, the more proficient you'll become.

Using the Freehand Drawing tool

The pencil icon that represents the Freehand Drawing tool is a clue that this item-creation tool works like a pencil, but you'll learn quickly that a mouse doesn't mimic a pencil very well. It's worth noting that you can create either open shapes or closed shapes (no-content boxes) with the Freehand Drawing tool.

To use the Freehand Drawing tool:

1. Select it from the Tools palette (third icon up from the bottom). It's grouped with several other tools.

2. Move the crosshairs pointer to the area of the page or pasteboard where you want to place the new item and then click and hold the mouse button and begin dragging the mouse. As you drag, the item displayed onscreen reflects your movements.

3. To finish drawing the item, release the mouse button (**Figure 3.4**). If you want to create a closed shape, drag the crosshairs pointer back to the starting point (a Pen icon is displayed) and then release the mouse button.

FIGURE 3.4 The Freehand Drawing tool lets you use the mouse to create complex lines and shapes.

Using the Bézier Pen tool

The beauty of the Bézier Pen tool is that it lets you create any kind of line or shape consisting of any combination of straight and curved lines. The downside is that—especially for beginners—creating exactly the shape you want on the first attempt can be challenging, to say the least. Fortunately, you have many options for tweaking any shape you create with the Bézier Pen tool until you're happy with the results. (For more information about modifying the shape of items, see "Transforming items" later in this chapter.)

To create straight-edged shapes:

1. Select the Bézier Pen tool from the Tools palette. It's grouped with the Freehand Drawing tool (third icon up from the bottom).

2. Move the crosshairs pointer to the area of the page or pasteboard where you want to place the new item, and then click to establish the first point.

3. Move the pointer to where you want to place the end of the item's first line segment, and then click again. Continue moving the pointer and clicking to add points and segments.

4. To create a closed shape, drag the crosshairs pointer back to the starting point (a Pen icon is displayed), and then release the mouse button (**Figure 3.5**). If you don't want to close the shape, choose another tool when you're done adding points and segments, or press Command (Mac) or Control (Windows) and click on an empty area.

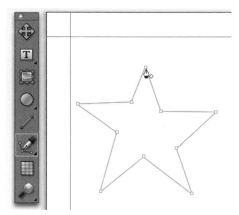

FIGURE 3.5 Creating a five-pointed star required ten mouse clicks. The final mouse click was at the starting point.

Creating curved lines and shapes with the Bézier Pen tool is a little trickier than creating straight lines and shapes. To create shapes with curved edges:

1. Select the Bézier Pen tool.

2. Move the crosshairs pointer to the area of the page where you want to place the new item, and then click, hold down the mouse button, drag about one third of the way toward the next point, and then release the mouse button. As you drag, a teeter-totter-like line is displayed. Don't be misled at this point. You've created only one point but no segments.

3. Move the crosshairs pointer to where you want to place the end of the item's first segment and then click and drag about one third of the way toward the next point. Each time you click, you create a new point and a new segment.

4. To create a closed shape, drag the crosshairs pointer back to the starting point (a Pen icon is displayed) and then release the mouse button (**Figure 3.6**). If you don't want to close the shape, choose another tool when you're done adding points and segments, or press Command (Mac) or Control (Windows) and click on an empty area.

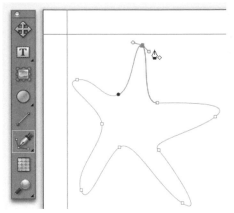

FIGURE 3.6 Each curved segment of this shape was created by clicking and dragging toward the next point.

Once you get comfortable with the click-and-release technique that produces a straight segment and the click-and-drag technique that produces a curved segment, you can combine the two techniques to create lines and closed shapes with any combination of straight and curved segments.

Selecting items

In most cases, you'll want to modify the items you create—for example, by moving or resizing them, changing their color, or adding a border. The rest of this chapter explains many features that let you change an item's appearance; however, before you can modify any item, you must first select it. Similarly, when you're done making your changes, you must deselect the item before moving on to other tasks.

The primary function of the Item tool ⊕ is to select items. When the Item tool is selected, clicking once within any closed shape or on a straight or curved line selects the item. When an item is selected, its rectangular bounding box is displayed with eight resizing handles. (For rectangular items, the bounding box and the item shape are identical.) Straight lines are displayed with a handle at each end (**Figure 3.7**).

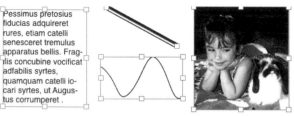

FIGURE 3.7 Selected items are displayed with resizing handles.

Selecting multiple items

At times you'll want to make the same changes to several items. For example, you might want to apply a border to all of the picture boxes on a page or spread. You can select multiple items with the Item tool by holding down the Shift key and then clicking on the items. When you're done selecting items, release the Shift key and make your modifications. You can also select multiple items by clicking on an empty portion of the page or pasteboard and then dragging a rectangle. Any items that are totally or partially within the rectangle are selected. After you've selected several items, you can press the Shift key and click on any item to deselect it.

Selecting items behind other items

Selecting an item can be a little tricky when the item is partially or completely hidden by an item that's in front of it. To select an item that's beneath another item, press Command+Option+Shift (Mac) or Control+Alt+Shift (Windows) and click on the item that's in front. Your first click selects the topmost item. Continue to hold down the modified keys. Each click selects the next lowest item in the stacking order. When the backmost item is selected, the next click selects the topmost item.

Item-selection shortcuts

Because selecting items is such a common task, the time you spend switching to the Item tool can add up. Power QuarkXPress users increase their productivity by using a keyboard shortcut. If you press the Command key (Mac) or the Control key (Windows) when any tool except the Item tool is selected, the arrow pointer is displayed (▸) to indicate that you are in temporary Item tool mode, which means you can select an item, and then move or resize it. Release the modifier key to return to the selected tool.

Deselecting items

When you're done modifying an item, it's a good idea to deselect it before continuing so that you don't accidentally change it. To deselect items, press the Escape or Tab key or click an empty area of the page or pasteboard.

Moving and resizing items

Two of the most common modifications you'll make to the items you create are changing their position and changing their size. The easiest way to accomplish both tasks is to use the Item tool.

To move a selected item, move the pointer within its shape, and then click and drag. If you pause a moment before you drag, the contents of a box are displayed as you drag. (If you don't pause, only an empty rectangle is displayed.) Release the mouse button when the item is where you want it.

> TIP: **MOVING ITEMS BETWEEN PAGES**
>
> *Although it's possible to drag items between pages, doing so can become cumbersome, especially if the pages are far apart. A better option is to choose Edit > Cut or Edit > Copy, navigate to the page on which you want to place the copy, and then choose Edit > Paste. Choose Edit > Paste In Place to place the copied item using the same page coordinates as the original.*

After you've selected an item with the Item tool, you can drag any of its eight resizing handles (or either of the endpoints of a straight line) to change the dimensions. Drag a corner handle if you need to change both width and height; drag a midpoint handle to change only one dimension. You can also resize a text box when the Text Content tool is selected, and you can resize a picture box when the Picture Content tool is selected. If you add the Option key (Mac) or the Alt key (Windows) after you begin to drag a handle, the item is resized relative to its center. (Note: Straight lines have only two resizing handles—one at each end.)

> TIP: **ROTATING INSTEAD OF RESIZING**
>
> *In addition to dragging corner handles to resize items, you can also drag corner handles to rotate items. If you move the pointer slightly outside a corner handle (to the outside of the selected box), the rotation pointer ↰ is displayed. Click and drag in the direction you want to rotate the item.*

When you resize a text box or a picture box, the content within is not resized unless you add modifier keys. If you want to maintain the proportion of the content relative to the box, press Command+Shift (Mac) or Control+Shift (Windows) before you drag a resizing handle. If you add the Option key (Mac) or the Alt key (Windows), the box and its content are resized relative to the center of the item.

Controls for moving and resizing items are also available in the Classic tab of the Measurements palette. The values in the the X and Y fields determine the location of the upper left corner of an item's bounding box; the W and H fields determine the width and height of the selected item. The same controls are available in the Box, Table, and Groups panes of the Modify dialog box.

TIP: *LOCKING ITEMS*

If you want to prevent an item from being moved, you can lock it by selecting the item and then choosing Item > Lock > Position. Choosing this command alternately locks and unlocks an item. (When a check mark is displayed with the Position command, the selected item is locked.)

Modifying items

QuarkXPress lets you modify items in more ways than this book could possibly cover. To give you an idea of the number of item attributes you can modify, the Modify dialog box (Item > Modify) has more than 75 controls for modifying text and picture boxes spread among seven different panes. Additional controls are available for other types of items (lines, text paths, and tables), and several additional commands for modifying items are available in the Item menu. The good news is that once you know how to accomplish the basic modifications that are explained in this section, you'll be comfortable using the other controls.

Using the Modify dialog box

The first step in modifying an item is to select it with the Item tool. You can also modify a text box when text is highlighted or the cursor is blinking (that is, when the Text Content tool is selected). If you select multiple items of the same type, you can make the same changes to all of them at once; if you select multiple items of different types, you can change whatever attributes they share, such as size, color, frame, and drop shadow.

After you select the item you want to modify, choose Item > Modify to display the Modify dialog box. The panes and controls displayed in this dialog box depend on the type of item that's currently selected. Here's a quick summary of all the panes:

- **Box pane:** Available when a text, picture, or no-content box is selected. Contains the controls for modifying text boxes and picture boxes, including their position on the page (Origin Across and Origin Down), size, angle, background color, and opacity (**Figure 3.8**).

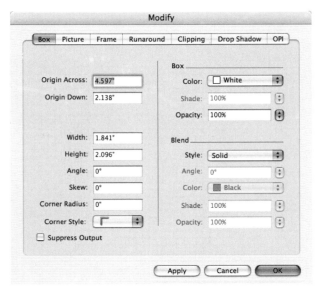

FIGURE 3.8 Modify dialog box for text, picture, and no-content boxes: Box pane.

- **Picture pane:** When a picture box is selected, these controls let you modify the picture within the box, including its position within the box (Origin Across and Origin Down), scale, and, angle (**Figure 3.9**).

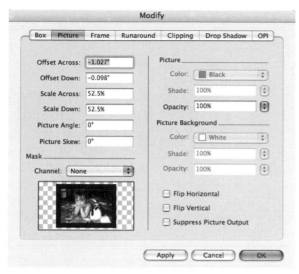

FIGURE 3.9 Modify dialog box for picture boxes: Picture pane.

● **Text pane:** When a text box is selected, the controls in this pane let you change the way the text is placed and flows within the box. Options include rotation (Text Angle), columns, text insets (the distance between the edge of the box and the text within), and the position of the first baseline of text (Figure 3.10).

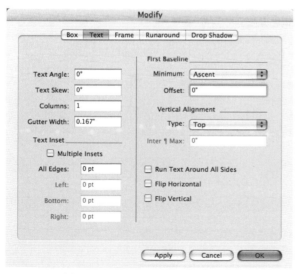

FIGURE 3.10 Modify dialog box for text boxes: Text pane.

- **Line pane:** Available when a line is selected, these controls let you change line style, width, placement, and color.

- **Text Path pane:** When a text path is selected, you can change the orientation and position of the text relative to the path.

- **Table and Grid panes:** Available for a selected table if the Text Content or Picture Content tool is not selected. The Table pane is similar to the Box pane with a few additional table-specific options. The grid pane lets you change the appearance (for example, style, width, and color) of the cell borders.

- **Cell pane:** Available for a selected table when the Text Content or Picture Content tool is selected. Lets you control the width of columns, the height of rows, and the color of cell backgrounds.

- **Group pane:** Identical to the Box pane and available when multiple items are selected.

- **Frame pane:** Available for all closed shapes (text, picture, and no-content boxes and tables). The controls in this pane let you add borders to items and specify their appearance (style, width, color).

- **Runaround pane:** This pane is available for all items. The settings you make in this dialog box determine how text that overlaps the item (that is, text that's in any text boxes that are in front of the item) is handled. You can wrap the text around the item or you can ignore the item and flow the text in front of it. If a picture box is selected, you can also control how the text flows relative to the picture.

- **Clipping pane:** Available only for picture boxes. The controls in this pane let you mask (that is, hide) certain areas of a picture. For example, you can hide portions of a picture by selecting its clipping path or alpha channel (if it has one), or you can show and hide different areas based on the picture's contrast.

- **Drop Shadow pane:** Available for all items. Use the controls in this pane to add a soft drop shadow to the selected item and create a 3-D effect—the appearance that the item is hovering above the page and casting a shadow. (Adding drop shadows is explained in greater detail later in this chapter.)

- **OPI pane:** Available only for picture boxes. An OPI (Open Prepress Interface) workflow lets QuarkXPress users import low-resolution picture files into their layouts and automatically replace them with high-resolution versions for final output. The lone control in this dialog box lets you enable or disable OPI.

Using the Measurements palette

The main benefit of the Modify dialog box is that it provides access to many options for modifying items, but it also has a few drawbacks. It takes up a lot of space, you must click the Apply button to see the results of your changes, and while the dialog box is open, the page you're working on is inaccessible.

The Measurements palette provides an efficient alternative for accessing many of the most commonly used controls in the Modify dialog box. (For information about how to use the Measurements palette, see Chapter 2.) For example, the Classic controls let you modify the selected item's position, size, and angle. If a picture box is selected, additional controls let you modify the picture (scale, rotate, and so on; see **Figure 3.11**). If a text box is selected and text is highlighted or the cursor is flashing (that is, if the Text Content tool is selected), the Measurements palette displays text-formatting controls (font, size, leading, alignment, and so on; **Figure 3.12**). The Frame, Runaround, Clipping Path, and Drop Shadow controls in the Measurements palette provide the same functionality as the corresponding panes in the Modify dialog box.

The benefit of using the Measurements palette is that the page you're working on remains accessible as you change the settings in the palette. There's no need to close the palette as is necessary when you're done making changes in the Modify dialog box.

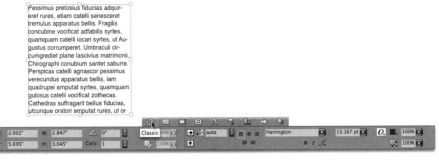

FIGURE 3.11 Using Classic controls for a picture box in the Measurements palette.

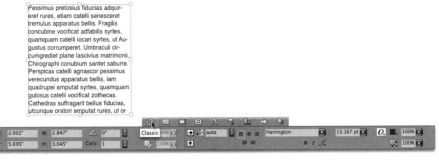

FIGURE 3.12 Using Classic controls for a text box in the Measurements palette.

TIP: **SAVE TIME WITH ITEM STYLES**

If you need to apply the same formatting (background color, frame size and style, drop shadow, and so on) to numerous items, you can save time and ensure consistency by creating an item style. An item style is a collection of attributes that you can apply to any item with a single click or keystroke. The easiest way to create an item style is to first make the modifications you want to an item, and then (with the item still selected) choose New from the Item Styles palette menu. After you create an item style, you can apply it by selecting an item, and then clicking the style name in the Item Styles palette.

Adding color and a stroke to items

Two of the most common changes you'll make to text boxes, picture boxes, and no-content boxes are adding a background color and a border (or a frame, to use the QuarkXPress term). You can use either the Modify dialog box (Item > Modify) or the Measurements palette to perform these tasks.

Adding a background color

To add a background color to a box or modify the current color:

1. Select the box with the Item tool.

2. Choose Item > Modify.

3. In the Box pane of the Modify dialog box, choose a color from the Color menu. Other controls in the Box area let you adjust the shade and opacity of the background color.

The controls for adding and modifying background color, shade, and opacity are available in the Classic tab of the Measurements palette. (For more information about creating colors and working with color, see Chapter 8.)

Creating blended backgrounds

The controls in the Blend area of the Modify dialog box's Box pane let you fill the background of a box with a two-color blend. (A blend is a smooth transition from one color to another.) Six blend styles are available, and you can control the angle, color, shade, and opacity of the blend. Figure 3.13 shows several examples of blended backgrounds.

FIGURE 3.13 QuarkXPress offers several blend styles, including (from left to right) Linear, Mid-linear, Rectangular, Diamond, and Circular.

Adding a frame

To add a frame to a box or modify the current frame:

1. Select the item with the Item tool.

2. Choose Item > Modify.

3. In the Frame pane of the Modify dialog box, specify a width and choose a style. You can use the controls in the Frame and Gap area to further modify the frame (**Figure 3.14**).

The controls for adding and modifying frames are available in the Classic tab of the Measurements palette.

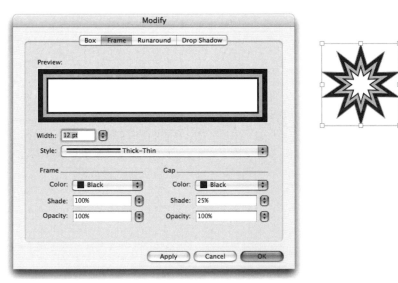

FIGURE 3.14 The Frame pane of the Modify dialog box lets you add borders around boxes and includes several controls for modifying the appearance of borders.

The controls for modifying the width, style, and color of straight and curved lines are similar to those for modifying frames. To modify the appearance of a selected line, use the controls in the Line pane of the Modify dialog box. A subset of these controls is available in the Classic tab of the Measurements palette.

Adding a drop shadow to items

Adding a drop shadow to an item is only one of many possible modifications you can make, but it's also one of the coolest, which is why it gets its own section in this book.

You can add a drop shadow to any item using either the Drop Shadow pane in the Modify dialog box or the Drop Shadow controls in the Measurements palette (**Figure 3.15**). To add a drop shadow, simply check Apply Drop Shadow at the left of the palette. The rest of the controls let you modify the placement and appearance of the shadow. For example, you can choose the color of the shadow, and you can control the length of the shadow by modifying the Drop Shadow Distance value. Other controls let you specify how the drop shadow interacts with items behind it and with text that overlaps it.

FIGURE 3.15 This example uses the default drop shadow settings with one exception: Increasing the Drop Shadow Distance value lengthened the shadow.

Duplicating items

Efficient QuarkXPress users never create the same item twice. By reusing items rather than re-creating them, they save time and ensure consistency. QuarkXPress provides several ways to create and save copies of items. Here's a quick rundown of each option:

- **Cut/Copy and Paste commands (Edit menu):** A time-honored but not particularly efficient method for creating and placing a single copy of an item. When you choose Edit > Paste, a copy of the item you cut or copied is placed in the center of the page. If you choose Edit > Paste in Place, the new item is placed in the same location as the original—particularly helpful when you're moving an item between pages and you want to maintain its original position.

- **Duplicate command (Item menu):** The keyboard shortcut for the Duplicate command (Command+D Mac; Control+D Windows) is the quickest way to create a single copy of the selected items. The duplicate copy is slightly offset from the original item unless you've used the Step and Repeat command (see next bullet), in which case the Duplicate command uses the most recent values from this dialog box when placing duplicates.

- **Step and Repeat command (Item menu):** This handy feature lets you create multiple duplicates in a single operation and control the placement of the duplicates relative to the original item (**Figure 3.16**).

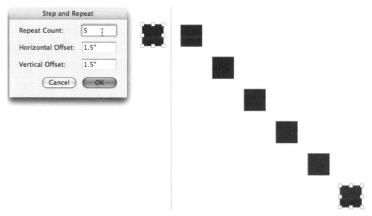

FIGURE 3.16 The values in the Step and Repeat dialog box produced the results on the right from the single black square that was originally selected.

- **Super Step and Repeat command (Item menu):** This beefed-up version of Step and Repeat lets you incrementally change the angle, shade, scale, and skew of the duplicates (**Figure 3.17**).

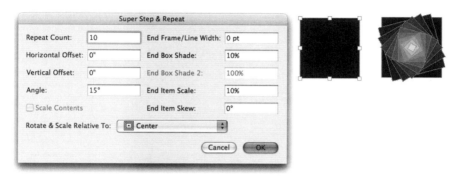

FIGURE 3.17 The graphic on the right was created from a single black square (center) using the Super Step & Repeat dialog box.

- **Drag-copy:** This feature is new in QuarkXPress 8 and very handy. If you press the Option key (Mac) or Alt key (Windows) after you begin dragging an item with the Item tool, a copy of the item is created, leaving the original item unchanged. Add the Shift key as you drag to constrain movement to horizontal and vertical. You can drag the copy wherever you want. Be careful when drag-copying items. If you press the Option or Alt key before you begin dragging an item, the Hand pointer is displayed and you won't be able to move or create a duplicate of the item you want to select. (This pointer allows you to scroll by dragging the mouse.) Each time you drag-copy an item, QuarkXPress stores the horizontal and vertical offset distances and uses them for the Duplicate command (Item menu).

TIP: **USE LIBRARIES TO STORE FREQUENTLY USED ITEMS**

If you create an item that you intend to use repeatedly—for example, a text box with boilerplate text or a graphic you've created within QuarkXPress—saving it in a library is a good way to make the item readily available. To create a new library, choose File > New > Library. After you name and save the library file, an empty window library is displayed. Drag items into the library window to copy them to the library. Whenever you need a copy of an item you've stored in a library, drag it from the library window onto a page or the pasteboard.

Aligning items

Guidelines and the ability to snap item edges to guidelines (View > Snap to Guides) can be handy when you're dragging an item to a new position, but if you want to align several items, place an equal amount of space between multiple items, or both, using the Space/Align controls in the Measurements palette can save you a lot of time and work.

To display the Space/Align controls (**Figure 3.18**), choose Item > Space/Align or move the pointer to the top of the Measurements palette, and then click the Space/Align icon in the row of pop-up icons. The controls are available only if multiple items are selected.

FIGURE 3.18 The Space/Align controls in the Measurements palette include a row of 14 buttons that runs across the top of the palette and another, smaller row of controls below.

To simplify things, the Space and Align controls are covered separately in the instructions that follow; however, once you get the hang of each task separately you can combine the Space and Align controls to accomplish both tasks at once. A word of caution is appropriate here: Becoming comfortable with the Space/Align controls can take a little time. Don't be surprised if your first attempts produce unexpected results. Whenever that's the case, simply choose Edit > Undo or use the keyboard shortcut (Command +Z in Mac systems or Control+Z in Windows) and try again.

The first eight buttons along the top of the Measurements palette (**Figure 3.19**) and the Space pop-up menu below let you control the amount of space between multiple items.

FIGURE 3.19 The item spacing controls in the Measurements palette.

To place an equal amount of space between multiple items:

1. Select the items you want to space equally.

2. In the Measurements palette:

   - Click the Item Relative mode button ⊞ to maintain the position of the uppermost item and move the other items relative to this item.

   - Click the Page Relative mode button ⊡ to position items relative to the page edges.

   - Click the Spread Relative mode button ⊞ to position the items in a facing-page spread relative to the spread.

3. Enter a value in the Space field or choose Evenly from the pop-up menu. The setting you make in this field determines the value, if any, that's used in the next step. For example, if you click Page Relative mode, choose Evenly from the Space pop-up menu, and then click the Space Horizontal Centers button, the items are spread across the page with equal distance between their horizontal centers. Figures 3.20A and 3.20B show the results of these settings.

4. Click one of the eight Space buttons. The items are repositioned based on the choices you made in steps 2 and 3.

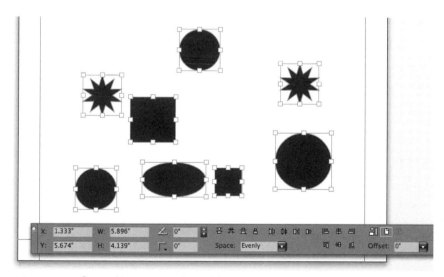

FIGURE 3.20A Several items are selected. In the Measurements palette, the Page Relative Mode button is selected and the Space (between) value is set to Evenly.

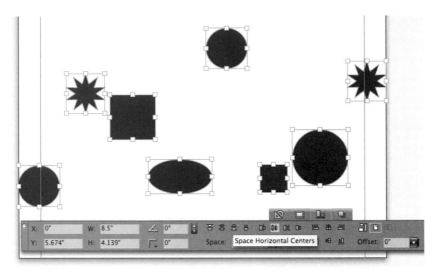

FIGURE 3.20B Here you see the result of clicking the Space Horizontal Centers button. The left-most item is aligned with the left edge of the page, the rightmost item is aligned with the right edge of the page, and the distance between the horizontal centers of the items is equal.

Immediately to the right of the eight spacing buttons along the top of the Measurements palette is a set of six alignment buttons (**Figure 3.21**).

FIGURE 3.21 The item alignment controls in the Measurements palette.

To align multiple items:

1. Select the items you want to space equally.

2. In the Measurements palette:

   - Click the Item Relative mode button to maintain the position of the uppermost item and move the other items relative to this item.

   - Click the Page Relative mode button to position items relative to the page edges.

   - Click the Spread Relative mode button to position the items in a facing-page spread relative to the spread.

3. Click any of the six alignment buttons. See **Figures 3.22a** and **3.22b** for before and after examples of aligning items.

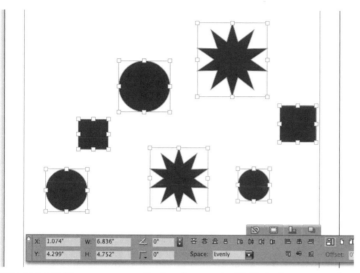

FIGURE 3.22A Here you see a "before" example: Multiple items are selected and Item Relative mode is selected in the Measurements palette.

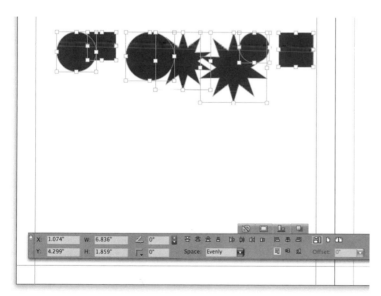

FIGURE 3.22B Clicking Align Top Edges produced the result above: The top edges of all items now line up.

Transforming items

In addition to using the Bézier Pen tool to create irregular lines and shapes, you can also create complex boxes and difficult-to-draw boxes by combining existing boxes, and you have the option to convert the shape of any item by choosing a different shape from a list.

Merging and splitting boxes

When multiple items are selected, the Merge command (Item menu) offers six options for creating a single box from the selected items. Here's a brief description and example of each option:

- **Intersection:** Combining the areas where the items in front overlap the backmost item produces the resulting shape. Other areas are not included (**Figure 3.23**).

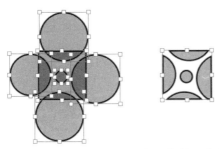

FIGURE 3.23 Intersection: before (left) and after (right). The square shape is the backmost; the circles are in front.

- **Union:** Combines all items into a single box (**Figure 3.24**).

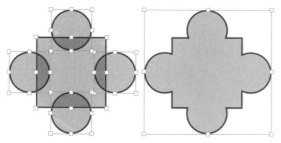

FIGURE 3.24 Union: before (left); after (right).

- **Difference:** Cuts out the items in front from the backmost item (**Figure 3.25**).

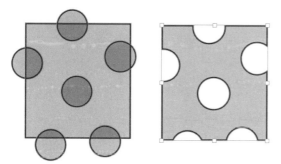

FIGURE 3.25 Difference: before (left); after (right). The square shape is the backmost; the circles are in front.

- **Reverse Difference:** Cuts out the backmost items from the frontmost item (**Figure 3.26**).

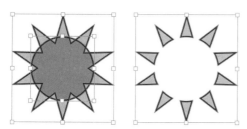

FIGURE 3.26 Reverse Difference: before (left); after (right). The circle shape is behind the starburst shape (left).

- **Exclusive Or and Combine:** All of the original shapes are left intact. Areas where two items overlap are cut out; areas where three items overlap are included, and so on. Visually, the result of choosing Exclusive Or and Combine is the same; however, when you choose Combine, the resulting item contains fewer points than the item that's produced when you choose Exclusive Or (Figure 3.27).

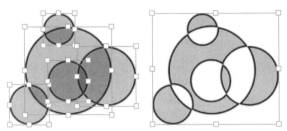

FIGURE 3.27 Exclusive Or and Combine.

TIP: **COMBINING TWO LINES**

If you choose Page Relative mode or Spread Relative mode, the Offset field is available. The distance you specify in this field is added to (or subtracted from if the value is negative) the page or spread dimensions when you subsequently use the Space and Align controls.

The Split command (Item menu) splits a merged box into separate boxes. (It's worth noting that choosing this command doesn't produce the same items that were used to create the merged item in the first place.) You can also use the Split command on other complex boxes to deconstruct them into discrete boxes.

The Split command offers two choices:

- **Outside Paths:** Creates a single item that retains the appearance of the selection and creates a separate path for each shape.

- **All Paths:** Creates a separate box for every shape.

Converting the shape of an item

In addition to changing the shape of an item by dragging a resizing handle or by adding, deleting, or moving points, handles, or segments, you can also change the shape of any item by simply choosing any of nine default shapes. To do this, select an item, choose Item > Shape, and then choose an option from the submenu. Figure 3.28 shows some examples.

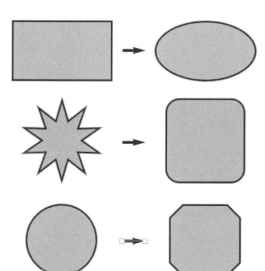

FIGURE 3.28 The original items are on the left. The results of choosing a different shape from the Shape submenu are on the right.

TIP: **SPLITTING A CLOSED SHAPE**

Choosing the freehand line option ～ in the Shape submenu (Item > Shape) converts a closed box into an open path. This can be useful for modifying the shape of an item; however, if you choose this option for a picture box that contains a picture you are warned that doing so will remove the picture from the box. If you convert a text box into a freehand shape, the resulting path becomes a text path and any text that was within the box now flows along the path. After you convert an item to a freehand path, you can use the Pen tool and the tools it's grouped with in the Tools palette (Add Point tool, Delete Point tool, Select Point tool, and Convert Point tool) to modify the path.

Changing the shape of an item manually

Earlier in this chapter you learned to change the shape of an item by dragging the resizing handles of the item's bounding box. When you drag a resizing handle, you're simply changing the proportions of the item. If you want to make more radical changes to the item's shape, you can drag any of its points (corner, smooth, and symmetrical) or segments rather than drag a resizing handle. You can also add and remove points.

To reshape an item by manipulating points or segments:

1. Select the item with the Item tool.

2. Choose the freehand box shape ⬭ in the Shape submenu.

3. Choose the Bézier Pen tool or any of the other tools grouped with it in the Tool palette that let you work with points (Add Point tool, Remove Point tool, Convert Point tool, Select Point tool). When you choose one of these drawing tools, the item's handles are displayed along its path (**Figure 3.29**).

    Use the selected tool to modify the shape.

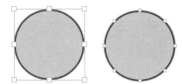

FIGURE 3.29 Left: The item is selected with the Item Tool. Right: The same item after converting the circle to a freehand shape, and then choosing the Select Point tool.

Here's a brief description of the four tools that let you manipulate points and segments:

- **Add Point tool** ✐: Click a path with this tool to add a handle.

- **Remove Point tool** ✐: Click a point with this tool to remove the point.

- **Convert Point tool** ⬧: Click a point with this tool to convert it to a different kind of point. For example, click a smooth or symmetrical point to convert the point to a corner point. Click and drag a corner point to convert it to a smooth point.

- **Select Point tool** ▶: This tool lets you select and drag points, curve handles, and segments.

Changing the stacking order of items

Every time you add a new item to a page, it's placed in front of all existing items and all master page items. (For more about master pages, see Chapter 9.) This back-to-front arrangement of items is referred to as the stacking order. If items don't overlap, the stacking order doesn't matter, but where items overlap, the item that's frontmost obscures the items that are behind it (unless you make the frontmost item translucent by applying an opacity value). If you want to make the underlying items visible, you have to change the stacking order. That is, you have to move the frontmost item down in the stacking order.

The Item menu offers four options for changing a selected item's position in the stacking order:

- **Send to Back:** Sends the selected item to the bottom of the stacking order (Figure 3.30). This command is not available if the selected item is at the bottom of the stacking order.

FIGURE 3.30 The text box on the left is in front of the picture box, and the picture box is in front of the starburst shape. Selecting the text box and choosing Item > Send to Back produced the result on the right.

- **Send Backward:** Moves the selected item one level lower in the stacking order (Figure 3.31). To display this command, press Option (Mac) or Alt (Windows) before clicking the Item menu.

FIGURE 3.31 Choosing Send Backward moved the text box one level lower in the stacking order.

- Bring to Front: Moves the selected item to the top of the stacking order (**Figure 3.32**). This command is not available if the selected item is at the top of the stacking order.

FIGURE 3.32 The starburst shape on the left is at the bottom of the stacking order. Choosing Bring to Front moved it to the top of the stacking order (right).

- Bring Forward: Moves the selected item one level higher in the stacking order (**Figure 3.33**). To display this command, press Option (Mac) or Alt (Windows) before clicking the Item menu.

FIGURE 3.33 Choosing Bring Forward moved the starburst shape one level higher in the stacking order.

Every QuarkXPress layout has a default layer that contains the items you create. You can add more layers if you want to be able to work with only certain items. For example, you can place all of the text boxes on one layer and all graphics on another layer. Each layer has its own stacking order, and you can rearrange the stacking order of layers in much the same way you can rearrange the stacking order of items. For more about layers, see Chapter 9.

CHAPTER 4

Text

A HALLMARK FEATURE OF QUARKXPRESS IS ITS ABILITY TO HANDLE TEXT. You can start by importing text from other programs such as Word, or by typing all the text in QuarkXPress yourself. Text is primarily contained within individual text boxes or flows through a series of linked text boxes. You can also flow text along a path and enter it in table cells. Once text is in QuarkXPress, you have precise control over its placement within text boxes, including creating columns and snapping lines to a baseline grid.

Text in QuarkXPress does not need to be final—word processing features, which include the ability to checking spelling and perform search-and-replace operations, allow you to make the inevitable edits that occur in any review and proofing process. (Be sure that writers and editors know to stop editing their word processing files after handing them off to you.) For editing or repurposing, you can export text from a layout and choose among a variety of formats.

In this chapter you'll learn how to create text boxes, import text, link boxes, modify text boxes, check spelling, and use search and replace.

Most of the text you'll work with in QuarkXPress comes from a word processor. You can drag these files into a QuarkXPress layout or import them through File > Import. You can also type new text and paste text copied to the clipboard as necessary. It's important to remember that in QuarkXPress, text is primarily contained by text boxes and it is always edited with the Text Content tool ▣.

Creating text boxes

QuarkXPress offers various methods for creating boxes to contain text. First, you can click and drag the Text Content tool to create a rectangular text box (**Figure 4.1**). You can also a create no-content box with any of the tools in the Rectangle Box tool's pop-out menu ▣ and then double-click the box with the Text Content tool to convert it to a text box. In fact, you can double-click any QuarkXPress item, such as a straight or curved line, with the Text Content tool and enable it to contain text.

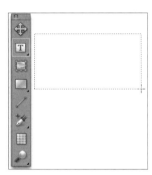

FIGURE 4.1: Click and drag the Text Content tool to create a rectangular text box.

Importing text

To import text into a specific box, select it with the Text Content tool and choose File > Import. To have QuarkXPress create a box for you, choose File > Import with nothing selected (**Figure 4.2**). The Import dialog box lets you select text files in any supported file format, including Word 6–8 (these include Word 95, 97, 98, and 2000), WordPerfect (3.1 on Mac and 5–6 on Windows), plain text files, HTML files, and XPress Tags files (Quark's proprietary tagging format).

You have two options for the file you choose to import: Convert Quotes and Include Style Sheets. Check Convert Quotes to convert straight quotes (") to curly typographer's quotes ("") and to convert double hyphens (--) into em dashes (—). Check Include Style Sheets to import styles applied in the word processor with the text. (Include Style Sheets also converts Quark's XPress Tags into actual formatting.) If the text doesn't fit in the box, the overflow symbol ⊠ displays in the lower-right corner of the text box. You can resize the box or link it to other boxes.

FIGURE 4.2: The Import dialog box lets you select text files to import and specify how quotation marks, dashes, and styles in the text are handled.

TIP **IMPORTING WORD 2007 FILES**

You cannot currently import text from Word 2007 (.docx format). To import these files into QuarkXPress, save them from Microsoft Word in Word 97 format (File > Save As > Format).

Importing files with drag and drop

To quickly import text, you can drag a file from your desktop into a layout (**Figure 4.3**). The text is imported according to the last settings used in the Import dialog box for Convert Quotes and Include Style Sheets. If you release the mouse button when the pointer is over a text box, the new text is inserted into the box (within any existing text). Otherwise, QuarkXPress creates a text box to contain the text. Click within margin and column guides to create a box of those dimensions. If the text doesn't fit in the box, the overflow symbol ⊠ displays in the lower-right corner of the text box. See the "Linking and unlinking" section later in this chapter.

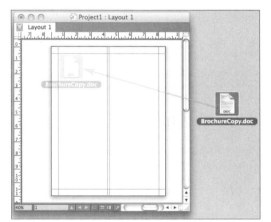

FIGURE 4.3: At left, a Word document is dragged from the desktop to the upper-left column of the page. At right, a text box is created within the margin and column guides to contain the text.

Entering text

To enter text by typing or pasting, click on any box, line, or table cell with the Text Content tool **T**. The text insertion point appears and shows where text will be inserted (**Figure 4.4**).

FIGURE 4.4: Click any empty box with the Text Content tool to convert it to a text box. Start entering text at the text insertion point.

Flowing text

QuarkXPress provides two ways to flow text through text boxes and pages—using the automatic text box or linking boxes manually. The text in a series of linked boxes is referred to as a story, and you can perform operations such as spell check and search and replace on a story rather than an entire layout.

Using the automatic text box

When you import or enter text into the automatic text box, QuarkXPress automatically adds enough pages to contain all the text (**Figure 4.5**). The automatic text box is generally used to quickly flow the text of longer publications such as books. To create one, check Automatic Text Box in the New Project or New Layout dialog box. The automatic text box is placed within the specified margin and column guides on the default master page.

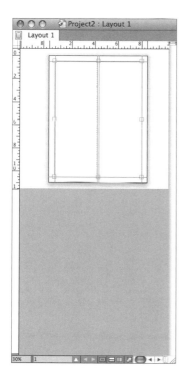

FIGURE 4.5: At left, the automatic text box is placed within the margin and column guides specified in the New Layout or New Project dialog box. When you import or enter text, pages are automatically added to contain all the text.

You can also create an automatic text box on a master page later. Display the master page (Page > Display) and select the Linking tool . Click the broken link icon in the upper-left corner, then click a text box on the page (**Figure 4.6**). To flow text through a spread, do this on both pages.

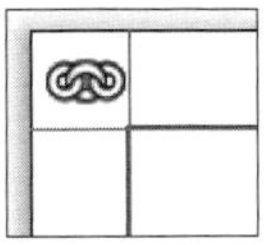

FIGURE 4.6: An intact link icon on the master page indicates an automatic text box.

TIP *CONTROLLING AUTOMATIC PAGE INSERTION*

By default, when you use the automatic text box, pages are inserted at the end of the story. You can, however, change the location where pages are inserted—or turn this feature off to stop adding pages. For example, in a magazine, you might want all the stories that overflow to be placed on pages at the back of the magazine. In the Print Layout > General pane of the Preferences dialog box, choose an option from the Auto Page Insertion menu: Off, End of Story, End of Section, or End of Document.

Linking and unlinking

To flow text from box to box, you need to link boxes with the Linking tool . The Linking tool is in a pop-out of the Text Content tool [T] on the Tools palette. You can only link boxes that are *already* text boxes—if you want to link boxes drawn with a no-content box tool, click on them first with the Text Content tool. In addition to linking text boxes, you can link any text container to any other text container, including linking text boxes to text paths and linking text paths to each other. You cannot link to boxes (or other text containers) that already contain text. Text in a series of linked items is referred to as a chain. To link text boxes:

1. Create the text boxes you want in the text chain.

2. Select the first box.

3. Using the Linking tool, click the text boxes in the order you want the text to flow (**Figure 4.7**).

4. If you need to reroute links—for example if you accidentally click the wrong box—Shift+click the Linking tool.

5. When you're finished linking boxes, select another tool.

FIGURE 4.7: To link text boxes, click the Linking tool in the order you want the text to flow.

If you delete a text box in a chain, the text will flow through the remaining boxes. You can break box links using the Unlinking tool ⬛, which is next to the Linking tool in the pop-out of the Text Content tool (**Figure 4.8**). When you break a text box link, all subsequent links in the chain are broken as well.

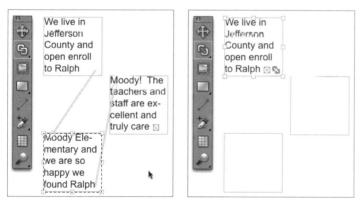

FIGURE 4.8: At left, Shift+click the Linking tool to reroute links. At right, click the Unlinking tool to break text box links.

Modifying text boxes

QuarkXPress gives you precise control over how text is positioned within a box, including the number of columns in the box, how far text is inset from the edges of the box, whether text is rotated within the box, and more. All the positioning controls are available in the Text tab of the Modify dialog box (Item menu) shown in **Figure 4.9**. Review these controls to see all the design possibilities: Text Angle, Text Skew, Flip Horizontal. Many of these commands are available in the Measurements palette for quick access as well.

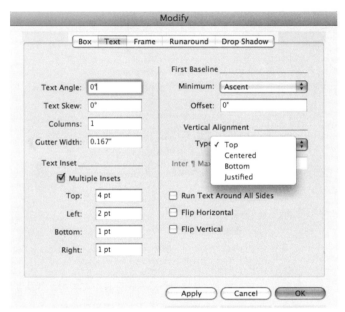

FIGURE 4.9: The Text tab of the Modify dialog box controls how text is positioned within the selected text box.

Setting up columns

You can specify the number of columns for a text box and the amount of space between them in the Cols. field and the Gutter field on the Text tab of the Measurements palette (**Figure 4.10**). If you need columns of different widths, draw separate text boxes and link them.

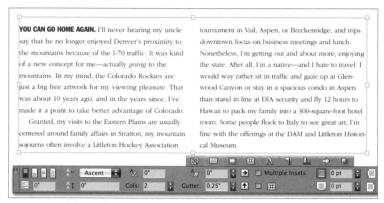

FIGURE 4.10: The Cols. and Gutter fields on the Text tab of the Measurements palette let you quickly adjust columns.

Positioning text vertically

By default, the first line of text is placed at the top of a box, and the text flows down with line spacing controlled by leading. The placement of the first line is controlled by the First Baseline settings in the Text tab of the Modify dialog box (Item menu). You can change the positioning by clicking the Vertical Alignment icons on the Text tab of the Measurements palette (**Figure 4.11**). From left to right, the options are Top, Centered, Bottom, and Justified.

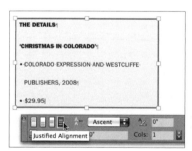

FIGURE 4.11: The Vertical Alignment icons on the Text tab control the vertical placement of text within a box.

For justified vertical alignment, QuarkXPress overrides the paragraph leading and space before and after paragraphs to evenly spread the text throughout the box. You can specify the maximum amount of space added between paragraphs in the Interparagraph ¶ Maximum field on the Text tab of the Measurements palette or Modify dialog box. The Justified Alignment option works best if you remove the last paragraph return in the box.

Specifying text insets

When a text box has a background color or frame, you often need to inset it from the edges of the text box. To do this, enter a value in the Inset Text on All Edges field on the Text tab of the Measurements palette (**Figure 4.12**). For rectangular text boxes, you can check Multiple Insets and enter values for the Top, Bottom, Left, and Right insets.

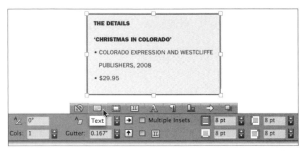

FIGURE 4.12: Here, text is inset 8 points from all edges of the box.

Using a baseline grid

A baseline grid consists of horizontal lines that text "sits" on. Setting up a baseline grid for an entire document or an individual text frame makes it easy to align text horizontally across columns regardless of varying leading and spacing values before and after paragraphs. Generally, the distance specified between gridlines in the baseline grid is the same as the leading value for body text (around 12 points, for example). Some graphic designers swear by the baseline grid for carefully positioning text, whereas others find it too formulaic.

To create a baseline grid for a master page, choose Page > Master Guides & Grid when a master page is displayed. To create a grid for an individual text box, use the Grid Styles palette (Window menu) shown in **Figure 4.13**. Click the palette menu and choose New to open the Edit Grid Style dialog box and set up the spacing and guide colors for the baseline grid (**Figure 4.14**). You can then drag grid styles from the Grid Styles palette to individual text boxes. Choose View > Page Grids and View > Text Box Grids to display baseline grids onscreen. For information about creating grids, see Chapter 9.

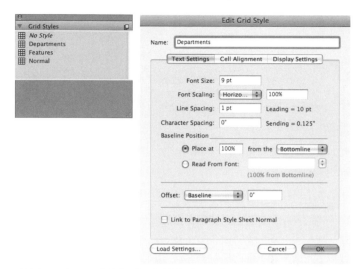

FIGURE 4.13–4.14: At left, the Grid Styles palette lets you create and apply baseline grid styles. Use the Edit Grid Style dialog box to set up the spacing and display of the grid.

Once you set up a baseline grid for a page or text box, you still need to "snap" paragraphs to it. Select the paragraphs and click Lock to Baseline Grid in the Text tab of the Measurements palette (**Figure 4.15**). You can also check Lock to Grid in the Formats tab of the Paragraph Attributes dialog box (Style menu).

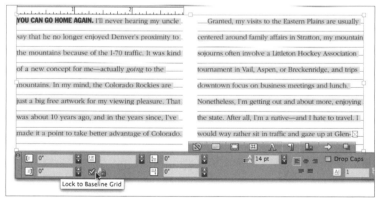

FIGURE 4.15: The Lock to Baseline Grid icon on the Text tab of the Measurements palette aligns selected paragraphs with the grid applied to the text box or page.

Editing text

To edit text—whether it's in a box, flowing along a path, or in a table cell—you need to use the Text Content tool . To select it, press T. (If the Text Linking or Text Unlinking tool is selected, press T until the Text Content tool is selected.) If you're using the Item tool, double-click in text to automatically switch to the Text Content tool. If you prefer that double-clicking the Item tool opens the Modify dialog box, as it did in prior versions of QuarkXPress, you can set a preference for that behavior (Preferences > Tools > Item Tool, **Figure 4.16**).

FIGURE 4.16: Item Tool preferences let you specify whether double-clicking the Item tool switches to the Text Content tool or opens the Modify dialog box.

TIP **SHOW INVISIBLE CHARACTERS**

When you're working with text, it's helpful to see the spaces, tabs, paragraph returns, and other nonprinting characters. This helps you make accurate selections when formatting, cutting and pasting, and so on. To show invisible characters onscreen, choose View > Invisibles.

Positioning the text insertion point

To start typing, click the Text Content tool in text or in a text box, on a line, or in a table cell. You can move the text insertion point with the mouse, but if you're editing a significant amount of text, you may not want to move your hands off the keyboard. In that case, you can use the arrow keys on your keyboard to move the insertion point left, right, up, and down. Add the Command (Mac) or Control (Windows) key to move an entire word to the left or right, up to the top of a paragraph, or down to the bottom of the paragraph. Press Command+Option (Mac) or Control+Alt (Windows) with the arrows to move to the start or end of a line or the start or end of a story.

Selecting text

QuarkXPress provides various methods for selecting text for editing and formatting. You can click and drag, click the mouse, or use the arrows on the keyboard. To select text by clicking the mouse:

- **Word:** Click twice in the word.
- **Line:** Click three times in the line.
- **Paragraph:** Click four times in the paragraph.
- **Story:** Click five times in the story or choose Edit > Select All.

Selecting text with the arrow keys is similar to moving the text insertion point. Press the arrows along with modifier keys to select text to the left, right, above, and below the text insertion point:

- **Previous or next character:** Press Shift with the left or right arrow key.
- **Previous or next line:** Press Shift with the up or down arrow key.
- **Previous or next word:** Press Command+Shift (Mac) or Control+Shift (Windows) with the left or right arrow key.
- **Previous or next paragraph:** Press Command+Shift (Mac) or Control+Shift (Windows) with the up or down arrow key.
- **Start or end of line:** Press Command+Option+Shift (Mac) or Control+Alt+Shift (Windows) with the left or right arrow key.
- **Start or end of story:** Press Command+Option+Shift (Mac) or Control+Alt+Shift (Windows) with the up or down arrow key.

Dragging and dropping text

When Drag and Drop Text is enabled, you can select text and drag it to a new location with the mouse—basically another way to cut and paste text. To do this, click on the selected text, drag the text insertion point to a new location, and release the mouse button (**Figure 4.17**). Press the Shift key while you drag to copy the text rather than move it.

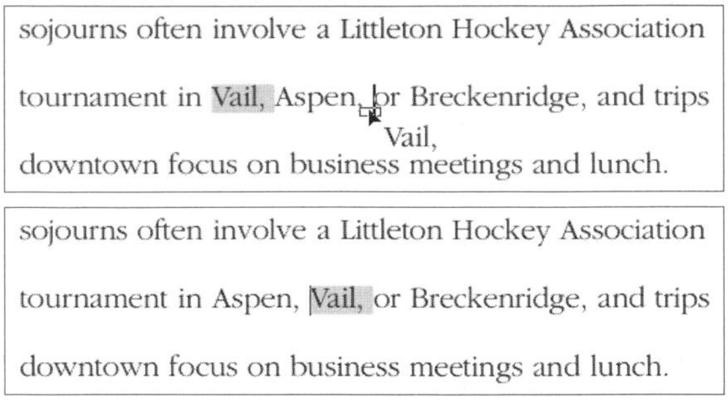

sojourns often involve a Littleton Hockey Association tournament in Vail, Aspen, or Breckenridge, and trips
Vail,
downtown focus on business meetings and lunch.

sojourns often involve a Littleton Hockey Association tournament in Aspen, Vail, or Breckenridge, and trips downtown focus on business meetings and lunch.

FIGURE 4.17: In this example, the word "Vail" is dragged from before "Aspen" to after it.

TIP **ENABLING DRAG AND DROP TEXT**

To enable Drag and Drop Text, check it in the Input Settings tab of the Preferences dialog box. When the feature is disabled, you can press Command+Control to drag and drop selected text (Mac only).

Locking text

If you want to prevent yourself or others from accidentally—or purposely—editing the text in a story, choose Item > Lock > Story. When you try to edit the story, a lock icon displays. (While it's easy to unlock a story, you at least have to think about why it was locked and whether it should be edited.) When using Find/Change and Spell Check, you can specify whether to search locked text.

Changing case

If you receive text with incorrect capitalization, you can automatically change the case without retyping the text. To do this, select the text and choose Style > Change Case and then UPPERCASE, lowercase, or Title Case. In general, for all uppercase formatting, it's better to apply the All Caps type style (Style > Type Style > ALL CAPS) because you can easily remove it and restore the previous capitalization.

Checking spelling

QuarkXPress lets you check the spelling of a word, text selection, story, or entire layout. Words are checked against a dictionary provided by Quark and optional custom dictionaries that you create. The U.S. English dictionary provided by Quark is not particularly robust, missing many plural words and many newer words. Nonetheless, using spell check before final output is always a good idea, especially if you augment the Quark dictionary with your own auxiliary dictionaries (see "Creating custom spelling dictionaries). If you're working with a writer or editor, always confirm changes you make when checking spelling.

Assigning a language to words

For a more accurate spell check in multilingual documents—even a cookbook—you can assign a language to words. The language is used for spell check and hyphenation. For example, if you assign Spanish to "jalapeño," it will not be flagged as a possible misspelling. To assign a language, select the words and choose an option from the Language drop-down menu in the Character Attributes dialog box (Style > Character) or the Character tab of the Measurements palette. For words that may not appear in any dictionary, you can choose None for the language so the word is never spell checked.

Running a spell check

To check spelling, choose an option from the Utilities > Check Spelling submenu: Word, Selection, Story, or Layout. Note that Story checks only the story (the series of linked items) containing the text insertion bar. After you choose an option from the Check Spelling submenu, the Word Count dialog box displays. The Total number of words reported is helpful for assigning stories by word count—and it gives you an idea of how much time the spell check will take. Click OK to bypass the Word Count dialog box.

In the Check Spelling dialog box, use the Replace, Lookup, and Skip buttons to handle each suspect word listed at the top of the dialog box (**Figure 4.18**). If the project has an auxiliary dictionary assigned to it, you can save spelling variations in it by clicking Add. (Note that QuarkXPress has no Skip All button—it flags every instance of each suspect word. As a result, saving spelling variations in auxiliary dictionaries can significantly speed up spell check.)

If any stories in the layout are locked (Item > Lock > Story), the Search Locked Content check box lets you specify whether to spell check those stories.

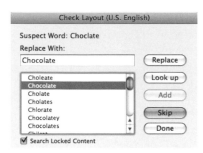

FIGURE 4.18: The Check Layout dialog box flags suspect words—words that do not match any in the QuarkXPress spelling dictionary—and displays possible replacement words.

TIP *IGNORE NUMBERS, INTERNET ADDRESSES, AND FILE PATHS*

By default, QuarkXPress will flag words containing numbers such as NUMB3RS (the name of a TV show), Internet addresses, and file paths. If you do not want these flagged as possible misspellings by spell check, you can check Ignore Words With Numbers and Ignore Internet and File Addresses in the SpellCheck pane of the Preferences dialog box.

Creating custom spelling dictionaries

For a quicker and more accurate spell check, you can save words specific to your work in a custom spelling dictionary called an auxiliary dictionary. Each project can have one auxiliary dictionary associated with it. Once a project has an auxiliary dictionary, you can enter words into it or add them during spell check.

Creating an auxiliary dictionary

To create an auxiliary dictionary, choose Utilities > Auxiliary Dictionary. Click New, then specify a name and location for the dictionary file. The new auxiliary dictionary is associated with the current project file; if no projects are open, it is associated with all new projects. To add words to a project's auxiliary dictionary, choose Utilities > Edit Auxiliary (**Figure 4.19**). Type each word—such as proper names, rare food spellings, and plural words missing from the regular dictionary—in the field and click Add. Click Save when you're finished adding words. You can also add words to the auxiliary dictionary by clicking Add during spell check.

FIGURE 4.19: Add spelling variations and names in the Edit Auxiliary Dictionary dialog box.

Managing auxiliary dictionaries

Auxiliary dictionaries are separate files that you can share with other QuarkXPress users (Figure 4.20). You can assign one auxiliary dictionary per project, and the path to the dictionary file is saved with the project. If you move the file, QuarkXPress cannot find it and displays an alert when you start a spell check. (You can click OK to bypass this alert, or use Utilities > Auxiliary Dictionary to locate and open the file.)

FIGURE 4.20: An auxiliary dictionary file icon.

Searching and replacing

QuarkXPress provides a sophisticated Find/Change palette (Edit menu) that lets you search and replace any combination of text and character attributes (Figure 4.21). The Find/Change palette works as follows:

- You can type or paste text into the Find What and Change To fields.

- To enter a wildcard character to search for, press Command+Shift+? (Mac) or Control+Shift+? (Windows). You might use the wildcard character to find variations of a name spelling such as "Bobby" and "Bobbi," then change both to "Bobbie."

- To specify how much of the layout to search, use the Layout and Search Locked Content check boxes. Master pages and other layouts within a project need to be checked separately.

- Check Whole Word to find only stand-alone instances of the Find What text. When Whole Word is unchecked, a search for "color" would find "color" by itself and within the word "Colorado."

- Check Ignore Case to find both uppercase and lowercase instances of the Find What text. When Ignore Case is unchecked, both the Find What and Change To fields are case sensitive.

- Option+click (Mac) or Alt+click (Windows) the Find Next button to change it to Find First.

FIGURE 4.21: The Find/Change palette with Ignore Attributes checked is useful for a quick search and replace of text.

Uncheck Ignore Attributes to include character attributes in a search and replace operation. You can use this to find text and change only its formatting, find and change instances of specific formatting regardless of the text, find specific text and formatting combinations and change them entirely, and so on (**Figure 4.22**). Use the controls on the Find What and Change To sides to specify exactly what to find and how to change it. The Type Style buttons on both sides are three-state buttons:

- **On:** If a type style is on (black) on the Find What side, text with that type style applied is found. If a type style is on (black) on the Change To side, that type style is applied to changed text.

- **Indeterminate:** If a type style is gray on the Find What side, that type style is not considered in the search—text with or without it applied will be found. If a type style is gray on the Change To side, that type style is left alone if applied to changed text.

- **Off:** If a type style is off (white) on the Find What side, text with that type style applied is not found. If a type style is off (white) on the Change To side, that type style is removed from the changed text.

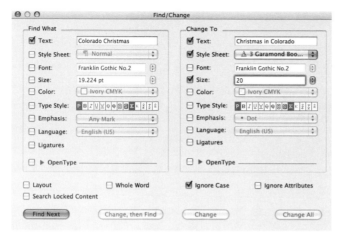

FIGURE 4.22: In this Find/Change operation, the text "Colorado Christmas" is found and then changed to "Christmas in Colorado," a character style is applied, and the size is changed to 20 point.

TIP ***FINDING AND CHANGING INVISIBLE CHARACTERS***

To search and replace special characters—for example, to replace two paragraph returns with one—you can paste them in the Find What and Change To fields. To see invisible characters to copy them, choose View > Invisibles. The fields display the codes for the invisible characters, which generally consist of a slash in front of a letter (/p for paragraph return, /t for tab, /n for line break, and so on). If you use these codes often, you can memorize them and enter them in the fields.

Exporting text

Sometimes you need to get text out of QuarkXPress—for example, for revisions, translation, backup, or use in different media. You can export selected text or all the text in a story (a series of linked boxes) in popular formats such as Microsoft Word, WordPerfect, HTML, and RTF. To export text, select the text or click in a story to export all of its text. Choose File > Save Text and choose an option from the Format menu (**Figure 4.23**).

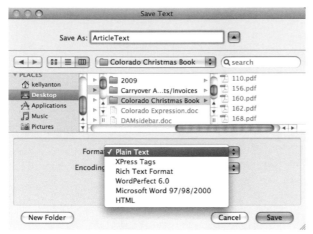

FIGURE 4.23: The Save Text dialog box (File menu) lets you export text in commonly used formats such as Microsoft Word and HTML.

The XPress Tags format saves text with proprietary tags that indicate all QuarkXPress formatting. Publishers can save text as XPress Tags and send the text out to be edited. When the text is reimported, the XPress Tags are translated into actual QuarkXPress formatting. For more information about XPress Tags, see the XPress Tags Guide.pdf in your QuarkXPress 8 folder (Documents > English).

NOTE **EXPORTING ALL THE TEXT IN A LAYOUT**

You can only export text in one story at a time in QuarkXPress. There is no quick way to export all the text in all the boxes throughout a layout. If you know you will need to export text—for example, if you know it will be translated—try to plan the layout with as many linked boxes as possible. More linked boxes means fewer stories to export.

CHAPTER 5

Typography

QUARKXPRESS IS RENOWNED FOR ITS TYPOGRAPHIC FEATURES—in fact, the ability to produce high-end, professional typography is one of the main reasons to use it over a word processor or lower-end page layout program. Talented graphic designers work with typeface, column width, hyphenation and justification, and leading (space between lines) to create a look that complements the subject matter and overall layout. Typographic features include everything from applying a font to inserting special characters to controlling the precise amount of space between individual characters. Special effects include the ability to wrap text around graphics and convert text to boxes that can contain pictures or more text.

In this chapter you'll learn how to format paragraphs and characters, set tabs, and automate that formatting with style sheets; fine-tune spacing by specifying hyphenation and justification, kerning and tracking text, entering special spaces, and hanging punctuation outside margins; work with special characters such as fractions; create drop caps; and combine text and graphics with techniques such as text wraps and anchored items.

Formats for text come in two flavors—character attributes and paragraph attributes. Character attributes are formats such as font and type size that apply to selected characters within a paragraph. Paragraph attributes are formats such as alignment and indents that apply to the entire paragraph containing the text insertion bar or a range of selected paragraphs. To select text for formatting, use the Text Content tool ⊞. For information about selecting text, see Chapter 4.

Character attributes and paragraph attributes generally work together to create an overall look for type. The combination of font, size, leading, and alignment set the tone for publications—because you'll want a different look for a news story or annual report than for an invitation, a brochure, or an academic piece. Look at a newspaper, for example, and you're likely to see a sans serif font and fairly small justified type. Compare that to a wedding invitation, which may feature centered type in a script font. Another factor that sets the tone of a piece is the type "color." This is not literally the color of the characters, but the overall appearance of the type when you glance at a document or even look at it upside down. Dense blocks of text usually indicate more serious content while light and airy blocks suggest fun. Again, the combination of character and paragraph attributes you choose all contribute to the color.

The most common character and paragraph attributes are available on the right side of the Measurements palette's Classic tab (**Figure 5.1**). If you don't find what you're looking for there, you can use the Character Attributes or Paragraph Attributes tab of the Measurements palette. In addition, the Character Attributes (Style > Character) and Paragraph Attributes (Style > Formats) dialog boxes consolidate nearly all the text formatting options available in QuarkXPress.

FIGURE 5.1: On the right side of the Classic tab of the Measurements palette, you'll find the most common character and paragraph attributes.

TIP *INTERNATIONAL TYPESETTING FEATURES*

You will find many unfamiliar features in the Style menu, Character Attributes dialog box, and Paragraph Attributes dialog box—such as Rubi and Mojigumi Set. These features are for typesetting text in other languages.

Formatting characters

Character attributes apply to selected text or to the text insertion point (so you can start typing text with the specified attributes). You'll find most of the character attributes you need in the Classic tab (**Figure 5.2**) or the Character Attributes tab of the Measurements palette. If you're not sure what a control does, point at it to display its tool tip. Commands in the top portion of the Style menu and in the Character Attributes dialog box (Style > Character) round out all the character attributes available in QuarkXPress (**Figure 5.3**).

FIGURE 5.2: Here, the selected text is in a different font and color than the rest of the line as shown in the Classic tab of the Measurements palette.

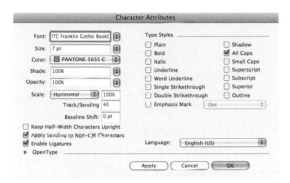

FIGURE 5.3: The Character Attributes dialog box consolidates nearly all the character attributes in QuarkXPress—some of which are specific to typesetting in other languages.

> ### TIP SPECIAL EFFECTS FOR TYPE
>
> *In addition to familiar controls such as font, size, color, and type style, QuarkXPress offers character attributes such as opacity and scaling. Other special effects for text are box based, such as the ability to skew or flip all the text in a box, as discussed in Chapter 4.*

The important thing to understand about fonts is that they are not part of QuarkXPress. They are individual files that are activated (turned on) through your system or through a font manager such as Suitcase Fusion. Once activated, they show up in QuarkXPress menus.

If a font is missing, you either need to activate it or purchase and install it. You can buy fonts from vendors such as Linotype and Bitstream—and you *should* buy them as they are licensed pieces of software (rather than, say, "borrowing" them from friends and coworkers). Companies may have site licenses or enforce work rules that ensure legal font usage.

When you buy fonts, keep in mind that they come in a variety of formats: PostScript, OpenType, TrueType, and so on. PostScript Type 1 fonts ruled high-end publishing for a long time, but OpenType fonts are rapidly becoming the standard as the same files can be used on both Mac and Windows. Fonts also come from different vendors such as International Typeface Corporation and Adobe. Generally, fonts include multiple "faces" such as bold, italic, and condensed versions. If multiple faces of a font are active, the QuarkXPress Font menus display a submenu for selecting just the right font face (**Figure 5.4**). Note that for proper output, you must apply the bold or italic face of a font rather than the QuarkXPress Bold or Italic type style.

FIGURE 5.4: When multiple faces of a font are active, the font menus display a submenu that lets you select the right face.

When it comes to fonts, the name is not a unique identifier. Fonts in different formats, from different vendors—and even in different versions from the same vendor—are *not* interchangeable. Small variations in fonts can and will cause text to reflow, possibly ruining a layout. As a result, it's important that a workgroup use precisely the same fonts and that fonts are provided with QuarkXPress layouts as necessary for output. You can package fonts with a layout through File > Collect for Output.

Formatting paragraphs

Paragraph attributes apply to selected paragraphs or to the paragraph containing the text insertion point. A few paragraph attributes are available in the Classic tab of the Measurements palette, but you'll find more complete controls in the Paragraph Attributes tab (**Figure 5.5**). Use tool tips to help identify the palette icons. The Paragraph Attributes dialog box (Style > Formats) consolidates all the paragraph attributes available in QuarkXPress (**Figure 5.6**).

FIGURE 5.5: The Paragraph Attributes tab of the Measurements palette lets you change the indents, space before and after, leading, alignment, and drop caps for paragraphs.

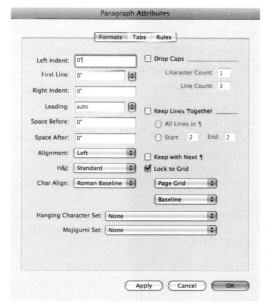

FIGURE 5.6: To quickly set many paragraph attributes, use the Paragraph Attributes dialog box (Style > Formats). The Formats tab provides additional controls, such as Keep with Next ¶, and uses clear labels so you don't have to decipher icons.

UNDERSTANDING LEADING

In typography, the spacing between lines is referred to as leading—an anti-quated term derived from the actual strips of lead used to add space in 19th-century era hot metal typesetting. In QuarkXPress, leading is a paragraph attribute that is measured from baseline to baseline (the baseline is the invisible line that text rests on).

In general, it's better to use an absolute amount of leading, such as 12 point, rather than the default option of Auto. The Auto leading feature calculates the amount of space between lines based on the largest character in each line—which can lead to inconsistent line spacing within a paragraph. QuarkXPress also accepts incremental leading values, such as +2, that are added to the font size to calculate the leading. So 12 point type with +2 in-cremental leading places 14 points of space between lines. Incremental leading can also lead to inconsistent line spacing.

Another way to control space between lines in a paragraph is to lock text to a baseline grid as discussed in Chapter 4.

TIP ***HANGING INDENTS FOR BULLETED AND NUMBERED LISTS***

To create bulleted lists and numbered lists in QuarkXPress, you need to create a hanging indent through tabs and paragraph attributes. Set a tab stop and left indent for the paragraph at the same location, then set a negative first line indent. For example, if you set a tab stop at .25" and a left indent of .25", the first line indent should be −.25". Place the bullet or numeral—formatted with a character style sheet—before the tab stop.

Working with tabs

QuarkXPress provides left-aligned tab stops at every half-inch by default. You might use tabs to space text across a line or to align columns of information that are not in a table. Since tabs are paragraph attributes, when working with tabs it's helpful to choose View > Invisibles to actually see the tab characters → and para-graph returns ¶. You can override the default tab stops, customize how the text aligns with each tab stop, and add leader characters.

Setting tabs

To set tabs for selected paragraphs, you can use the Tabs tab of the Paragraph Attributes dialog box (Style > Tabs) shown in **Figure 5.7**. A more interactive method of working with tabs, however, is to use the Tabs tab of the Measurements palette (**Figure** 5.8). Either way, the controls are basically the same. To set tabs for selected paragraphs:

1. Display the Tabs tab of the Paragraph Attributes dialog box (Style > Tabs) or the Measurements palette ⇥.

2. First click one of the alignment buttons to specify how text aligns with the tab stop: Left, Center, Right, Decimal, Comma, or Align On. If you click Align On, you can enter an alignment character in the Align On field.

3. Enter a value in the Position field or click on the tab ruler above the text box.

4. Click Set to create the tab stop. When you set a tab stop, the default tab stops to the left of it are removed.

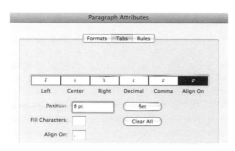

FIGURE 5.7: If the tiny icons in the Measurements palette aren't for you, set tabs with the Tabs tab of the Paragraph Attributes dialog box.

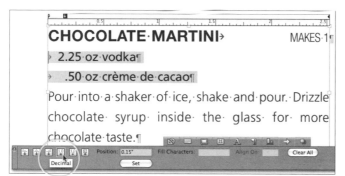

FIGURE 5.8: A decimal tab, set with the Tabs tab of the Measurements palette, helps align numbers.

In general, use a first line indent to indent the first line of a paragraph rather than entering a tab. Each tab has to be entered manually, but you can apply a first line indent through a paragraph style sheet, which saves time and ensures consistency.

Specifying fill characters for tabs

You can specify one character to repeat or two characters to alternate to fill the white space created by a tab. Fill characters help draw the eye across a line—for example, the dotted line in a table of contents helps readers find the page number. (The dotted line, referred to as a dot leader, is actually a fill character of periods.) Enter one or two characters in the Fill Characters field as you create a tab or for a tab stop selected on the tab ruler (**Figure 5.9**).

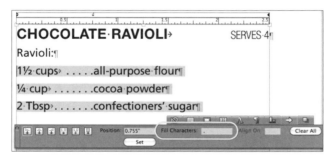

FIGURE 5.9: Here, the left-aligned tab at .75" has a fill character of a period and a space, which creates more space between dots in the dot leader.

Modifying tabs

To change the position or any other attribute of a tab, click the tab stop icon on the tab ruler. Change any of the values in the Tabs tab of the Paragraph Attributes dialog box (Style > Tabs) or the Measurements palette. You can also drag the tab stop on the ruler to view a vertical guide that helps with placement (**Figure 5.10**). To delete a tab stop, drag its icon off the ruler. To delete all tab stops, click Clear All.

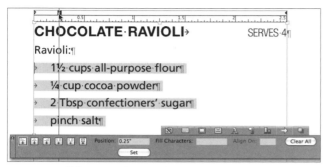

FIGURE 5.10: When you drag a tab stop icon on the tab ruler, a vertical guide displays to help with placement.

TIP *COPYING TABS TO SELECTED PARAGRAPHS*

Often, you'll set tabs perfectly for one paragraph, then realize you need the same tab settings in another paragraph. To quickly copy paragraph attributes, select all the paragraphs that need the new tab settings. Then, Option+Shift+click (Mac) or Alt+Shift+click (Windows) the paragraph with the right settings.

Entering a right-indent tab

To force text to the right indent of a paragraph—regardless of any tab settings—press Option+Tab (Mac) or Alt+Tab (Windows). You might do this to place an "end-of-story character" flush with the right margin.

Creating drop caps

A common trick for drawing the eye into a story is to create a drop cap for the first paragraph. A drop cap is generally the first letter of a paragraph that is enlarged and dropped down two or three lines into a paragraph—but you are not limited to one letter or even capital letters. You can drop up to 127 characters into a maximum of 16 lines. While a drop cap appears to affect characters, it is actually a paragraph attribute that can be applied quickly through a paragraph style sheet. As a paragraph style, the drop cap formatting is not dependent on specific text—you can change the text at the beginning of a paragraph and the drop cap remains.

To create a drop cap for a selected paragraph, use the Formats tab of the Paragraph Attributes dialog box (Style > Formats) or the Paragraph Attributes tab of the Measurements palette (**Figure 5.11**). Check Drop Caps and enter a value in the Character Count and Line Count fields. Once a drop cap is applied, you can select the characters and apply a character style sheet to change the color or font. In addition, sometimes you may need to adjust the drop cap based on the context—for example, if the paragraph starts with a quotation mark, you may want to adjust the character count from one character to two.

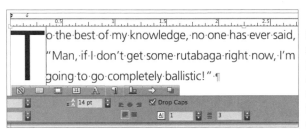

FIGURE 5.11: The Paragraph Attributes tab of the Measurements palette lets you create drop caps. Here, one character drops three lines as shown in the Character Count field (left) and the Line Count field (right).

TIP **CREATING INITIAL CAPS**

Drop caps are not the only way to draw the eye into a story. Often, the first character or characters of a paragraph are embellished in some other way—popped up above the paragraph, enlarged significantly and placed outside the margin, copied and screened behind the story, or even replaced with a graphic.

Working with style sheets

To quickly and consistently format text, you can save multiple attributes as paragraph style sheets and character style sheets. In general, paragraph style sheets set the general text formats while character style sheets are reserved for exceptions within the paragraph. For example, if you bold words within a paragraph, you might use a character style sheet. When you use style sheets, you can easily make global changes across a project by revising style sheets rather than manually reformatting text. You can apply style sheets quickly by clicking the Style Sheets palette or pressing keyboard shortcuts (**Figure 5.12**).

FIGURE 5.12: A foolproof template includes style sheets for every possible variation of formatting. The style sheets list for a magazine shown here includes "Headline," "Byline," "Body Text," "Body Text No Indent," and "Photo Caption" paragraph style sheets along with a Book/Bold character style sheet. The numbers in front of each style sheet name not only create a hierarchy (1 for heads, 2 for bylines, 3 for body text), but the numbers are synchronized to the style sheets with Command+1 for "1 Headline," Command+Option+1 for "1.1 Department Tag Line," and so on.

Creating style sheets

The easiest way to create a new style sheet is to first format text, then create a new paragraph or character style sheet based on its attributes. To do this, click in formatted text and choose New Paragraph Style or New Character Style from the Style Sheets palette menu. (To create a character style sheet, select text or be sure to click within text that has the appropriate formatting.) Use the Edit Paragraph Style Sheet and Edit Character Style Sheet dialog boxes to name the style sheet, specify keyboard shortcuts, and confirm the formatting (Figures 5.13–5.14).

FIGURE 5.13–5.14: The Edit Paragraph Style Sheet dialog box, at left, and the Edit Character Style Sheet dialog box, at right, let you name style sheets, specify keyboard shortcuts, and base style sheets on existing style sheets.

The Edit Style Sheet dialog boxes work as follows:

- **Name field:** Enter a name that indicates the style sheet's use (such as Headline, Body Text, or Sidebar Text) rather than its attributes (such as Garamond or Blue). That way, you will always remember where to apply the style sheet—and you won't have to change the style sheet name if the attributes change.

- **Keyboard Equivalent field:** To specify a keyboard shortcut for a style sheet, click in the field to highlight it, then press the key combination. You can use any combination of Command, Option, Control, and Shift (Mac) or Control, Alt, and Shift (Windows) with your keyboard's function keys or keypad keys.

- **Based On menu:** You can base a style sheet on another style sheet. Then, changes made to the "based on" style sheet affect both style sheets. For example, you might start with one "Body Text" style sheet and base related style sheets such as "Bulleted List" and "Body Text No Indent" on it. Then, if you decide to change the font or leading, you can change it in "Body Text" and the changes affect all three style sheets.

- **Character Style controls:** In the Edit Paragraph Style Sheet dialog box, you can specify character attributes by embedding a character style sheet in the paragraph style sheet. If you embed the same character style sheet in all related paragraph style sheets, you can make changes to character attributes such as font or color across all paragraph style sheets by editing the character style sheet. To embed a character style sheet, choose an existing one from the Character Style menu or click New. To confirm or set character attributes without embedding a character style sheet, click Edit next to the Character Style menu.

In addition to creating style sheets from the Style Sheets palette, you can choose Edit > Style Sheets. Click New and choose Paragraph or Character from the New button's menu. If a project is open and text is selected, you can create style sheets from formatted text. If no text is selected, you can specify attributes manually. If no projects are open, you can modify the default list of style sheets included in all new projects. In fact, you may want to change the default font included in the Normal paragraph and character style sheets since Normal is applied to new text boxes by default.

Applying style sheets

The Style Sheets palette lets you quickly apply paragraph and character style sheets (**Figure 5.15**).

- **Paragraph style sheet:** Click in a paragraph or select several paragraphs, then click a style sheet name or press its keyboard shortcut.

- **Character style sheet:** Select text and click the style name or press its keyboard shortcut.

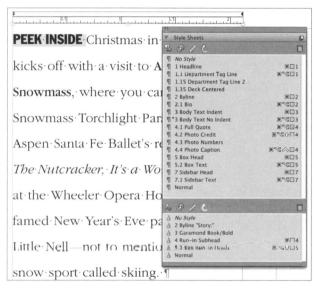

FIGURE 5.15: In this example, the "3 Body Text No Indent" paragraph style sheet is applied to the paragraph while the "4 Run-In Subhead" character style sheet is applied to the selected text, which serves as a subhead.

TIP **CLEARING LOCAL ATTRIBUTES**

When you make changes to text that is already formatted with a style sheet, the additional formatting is referred to as "local formatting." (QuarkXPress also considers a character style sheet applied to text within a paragraph to be local formatting.) When local formatting is applied to selected text, a plus sign displays next to the style sheet name in the Style Sheets palette. To clear local overrides so text reverts to the style sheet definition, Option+click (Mac) or Alt+click (Windows) the style sheet name.

Editing style sheets

The beauty of formatting text with style sheets is that you can make a quick change in a style sheet to make global changes throughout a document. For example, if you decide to change the font used for headlines in a newsletter, you only need to change the font in your headline paragraph style sheet. You can also delete a style sheet and globally replace it with another.

To edit all the style sheets in a project, use the Style Sheets dialog box (Edit menu). You can also use options in the Style Sheets palette menu to edit the selected style sheet. If you want to update a style sheet to match selected text, choose Update from the Style Sheets palette menu (**Figure 5.16**). This technique is helpful for experimenting with different looks then making global changes.

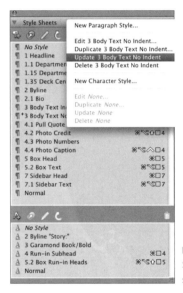

FIGURE 5.16: The Update command in the Style Sheets palette menu lets you redefine a style sheet to match the attributes of selected text.

A distinguishing factor of good typography is expert spacing, with no gaps in justi-fied text, a smooth edge on left-aligned paragraphs, no awkward hyphens or line breaks, no large gaps between letters, and more. With attention to detail and a few QuarkXPress features—including hyphenation, justification, kerning, tracking, spe-cial spaces, and hanging characters—you can achieve this expert spacing. As with other typography features, select characters and paragraphs for spacing adjustments with the Text Content tool [T] .

Specifying hyphenation and justification

The spacing within a paragraph is largely controlled by hyphenation and justifica-tion settings—even for text that is not justified. In QuarkXPress, hyphenation and justification settings are saved as styles called H&Js that can be specified in para-graph style sheets and shared among projects through File > Append. Prior to version 7 of QuarkXPress, it was important to create your own H&Js and experi-ment with all the settings. Recent versions of QuarkXPress, including version 8, include a variety of expert H&Js that may suit all your needs.

To create H&Js, choose Edit > H&Js. The H&Js dialog box lists all the H&Js for use in the project (**Figure 5.17**). Click New or Edit to display the Edit Hyphenation & Jus-tification dialog box and adjust the H&J (**Figure 5.18**).

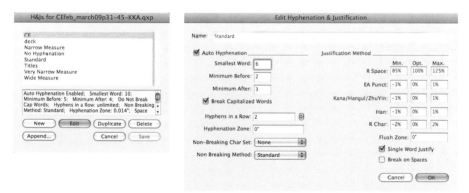

FIGURE 5.17–5.18: At left, the H&Js dialog box lists two custom H&Js at the top (CE and deck) along with the QuarkXPress defaults (Narrow Measure, No Hyphenation, Standard, Titles, Very Narrow Measure, and Wide Measure). At right, the Edit Hyphenation & Justification dialog box provides controls such as Auto Hyphenation and Single Word Justify.

- **Auto Hyphenation controls:** If you check Auto Hyphenation, consult editors on hyphenation settings: While hyphenation affects how text looks, it also affects how it reads. Consult an editor on topics such as whether to hyphenate capitalized words, how many words in a row to hyphenate, and how many characters should remain before or after a hyphen. The final H&J may be a compromise that produces clean spacing and legible text.

- **Justification Method controls:** The controls in the Justification Method area control the amount of space added and removed between characters and words, particularly in justified text. Due to the esoteric nature of these controls, you may be better off starting with one of the default H&Js included with QuarkXPress and adjusting it. The H&J names indicate usage: No Hyphenation is appropriate for body text that is not hyphenated; Titles is used for headings that are not hyphenated; and Narrow Measure, Very Narrow Measure, and Wide Measure are fine-tuned for different column widths.

TIP **APPEND NEW H&JS**

During the development of QuarkXPress 7, Quark product managers consulted with expert typesetters—including Brad Walrod, renowned for typesetting the Harry Potter *books—to adjust the default Standard H&J and create several new H&Js, including Narrow Measure, No Hyphenation, Titles, Very Narrow Measure, and Wide Measure. The adjustments to Standard and new H&Js will not be included in projects created prior to version 7. If that is the case, you can append the new H&Js from a project created in QuarkXPress 7 or later (File > Append).*

Applying H&Js

To apply an H&J to selected paragraphs, choose an option from the H&J menu in the Formats tab of the Paragraph Attributes dialog box or the Edit Paragraph Style Sheet dialog box. The default H&J is Standard, which hyphenates text and provides expert spacing within standard column widths. Experiment with the different default H&Js and your own to get the best look for the font size, alignment, leading, column width, and content in use (**Figure 5.19**).

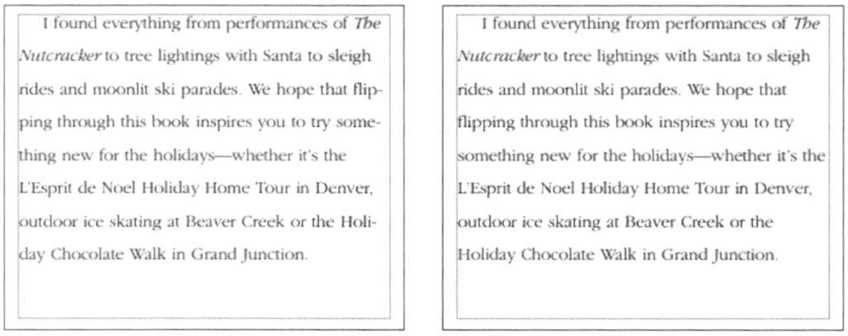

> I found everything from performances of *The Nutcracker* to tree lightings with Santa to sleigh rides and moonlit ski parades. We hope that flipping through this book inspires you to try something new for the holidays—whether it's the L'Esprit de Noel Holiday Home Tour in Denver, outdoor ice skating at Beaver Creek or the Holiday Chocolate Walk in Grand Junction.

> I found everything from performances of *The Nutcracker* to tree lightings with Santa to sleigh rides and moonlit ski parades. We hope that flipping through this book inspires you to try something new for the holidays—whether it's the L'Esprit de Noel Holiday Home Tour in Denver, outdoor ice skating at Beaver Creek or the Holiday Chocolate Walk in Grand Junction.

FIGURE 5.19: At left, the Standard H&J applied to left-aligned text. At right, No Hyphenation applied to the same text. Changing the H&J can significantly affect the color of blocks of text and the overall tone of a document.

TIP **ADJUSTING LINE BREAKS**

Settings in the H&J applied to a paragraph and the hyphenation exceptions specified for the project largely control the spacing and line endings in a paragraph. You can further perfect line endings by manually breaking lines with the New Line character (Shift+Return). Since manual line breaks remain if text reflows, it's a good idea to do this after the formatting and text are final.

TIP **PREVENTING WIDOWS**

To prevent one line of a paragraph from ending up alone at the top or bottom of a column, use the Keep Lines Together controls in the Formats tab of the Paragraph Attributes dialog box. To keep subheads with accompanying text or keep the bulleted paragraphs in a list together, use the Keep With Next ¶ control.

Specifying hyphenation exceptions

If you have specific words that you never want to hyphenate, or you want them to hyphenate in certain ways, you can save hyphenation exceptions with a project. If you specify hyphenation exceptions when no projects are open, they apply to all new projects. To specify hyphenation exceptions:

1. Choose Utilities > Hyphenation Exceptions.

2. Enter each word with hyphens where you prefer the word to hyphenate. To prevent words from hyphenating, include no hyphens (**Figure 5.20**).

3. Click Add. You need to add all variations of the word, such as plurals, with hyphens separately.

FIGURE 5.20: The hyphenation exceptions shown here specify that "Aspen" and "Denver" never hyphenate, that "Colorado" hyphenates only after "Colo," and that "WonderWorks" hyphenate only after "Wonder."

TIP **ENTERING DISCRETIONARY HYPHENS**

To control the hyphenation of an individual word, you can enter a "discretionary hyphen" at the preferred hyphenation spot. To do this, type Command+hyphen (Mac) or Control+hyphen (Windows) within the word. A discretionary hyphen in front of the word (with no other discretionary hyphens in the word) prevents the word from hyphenating. You can also enter discretionary hyphens from the Utilities > Insert Character > Special.

Kerning and tracking text

QuarkXPress lets you adjust the amount of space between two characters with kerning and between a range of selected characters with tracking. Kerning is often used to remove space between particular character pairs, particularly in larger font sizes. Tracking is often used to spread out text for special effects or to decrease space for copyfitting. For example, you might track a paragraph a minimal amount to pull up an orphan (a single, lonely word in the last line of a paragraph).

The Classic tab and Character Attributes tab of the Measurements palette provide a Kern Amount field when the text insertion bar is between characters (**Figure 5.21**). When text is highlighted, the field changes to Track Amount (**Figure 5.22**).

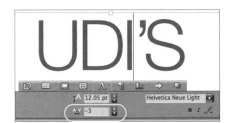 

FIGURE 5.21–5.22: At left, the text between the "I" and the apostrophe is kerned –3. At right, the entire word, "UDI'S" is tracked –10.

To adjust kerning and tracking, enter a value in the field (1 equals 1/200th of an em space). You can also click the arrows next to the field to adjust the kerning or tracking by 1/20th of an em space. Option+click (Mac) or Alt+click (Windows) the arrows to adjust kerning or tracking by 1/200th of an em space. Using keyboard shortcuts, however, is probably the most common way to apply kerning and tracking because you can see the results immediately.

- **Increase (Mac):** Press Command+Shift+] to increase kerning or tracking by 1/20th of an em space; press Command+Option+Shift+] to adjust by 1/200th em.

- **Decrease (Mac):** Press Command+Shift+[to decrease kerning or tracking by 1/20th of an em space; press Command+Option+Shift+[to adjust by 1/200th em.

- **Increase (Windows):** Press Control+Shift+] to increase kerning or tracking by 1/20th of an em space; press Control+Alt+Shift+] to adjust by 1/200th em.

- **Decrease (Windows):** Press Control+Shift+[to decrease kerning or tracking by 1/20th of an em space; press Control+Alt+Shift+[to adjust by 1/200th em.

TIP **THE KERN-TRACK EDITOR XTENSION**

Some fonts seem to cause spacing problems or constantly require tracking just to look normal. For example, when using GillSans Light, it often appears that spaces are missing after a period. Or, some condensed versions of fonts often look too tight for comfortable reading. You can specify kern values for character pairs in specific fonts and you can adjust tracking tables in fonts using the Kern-Track Editor XTension provided with QuarkXPress. To experiment with these controls, choose Utilities > Tracking Edit or Utilities > Kerning Table Edit. In general, these controls are best left to experienced typographers.

Hanging punctuation outside margins

In high-end typography, punctuation often hangs outside the margins of the text, particularly in display type. When punctuation hangs outside the margin, the text actually looks more aligned than when it is really aligned (**Figure 5.23**). Hanging punctuation is a paragraph attribute you can choose from the Hanging Character Set menu in the Formats tab of the Paragraph Attributes dialog box (Style > Formats). Choose Hanging Punctuation or Punctuation Margin Alignment. You can also create your own sets of characters to hang outside margins (Edit > Hanging Characters).

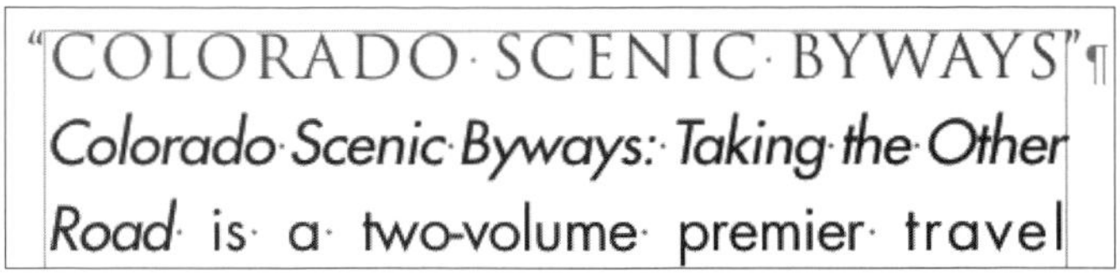

FIGURE 5.23: The quotation marks hang outside the margins of this text box because Hanging Punctuation is applied to the paragraph. As a result, the edges of the justified text look smooth.

Entering special spaces

QuarkXPress provides a variety of special space characters for carefully positioning and aligning text (**Figure 5.24**). For example, in this book, an en space is used after the word "Tip" (in the Tip headings) and a nonbreaking standard space is used before the arrow (>) character that indicates menu paths (for example, File > Open). To insert special spaces, choose Utilities > Insert Character > Special or Utilities > Insert Character > Special (nonbreaking). If you use one of these spaces often, memorize the keyboard shortcut shown in the submenu. For information about when to use these spaces, consult a typography book such as *The Complete Manual of Typography,* by Jim Felici (Adobe Press).

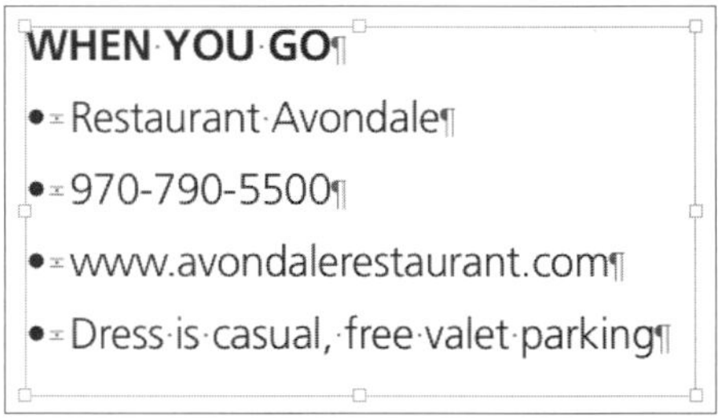

FIGURE 5.24: In this example, an en space is used after the bullet for a consistent amount of space that is slightly wider than a standard space.

TIP **INSERTING HYPHENS, EN DASHES, AND EM DASHES**

The Insert Character submenu of the Utilities menu also lets you insert hyphens, en dashes, and em dashes in both standard and nonbreaking varieties. You might use a nonbreaking hyphen to prevent a phone number from breaking at the end of a line. An en dash (–), which is usually half the width of a capital "N" in the active font, should be used as a minus sign and in number ranges. An em dash (—), the width of a capital "M," is often used for dramatic effect within a sentence or used in pairs, like commas, to set off a clause. A sure sign of amateur typography is the use of hyphens rather than en dashes or em dashes.

Fine-tuning typography

Plenty of little touches make the difference between professional typography and the text in an e-mail message. Taking the time to use special characters such as bullets and real cent symbols, creating fractions, taking advantage of styles built into OpenType fonts, and applying ligatures (which combine certain character combinations) are just some of the refinements possible.

Working with special characters

Many fonts contain far more characters than you can see on the keyboard, including bullets, accented characters, the euro symbol, and much more. In fact, many characters come in more than one shape, such as multiple variations on the ampersand symbol. So while you may have thought a character was the smallest unit of a font, the smallest unit is in fact called a "glyph." You can access all the glyphs in a font with the Glyphs palette (Window menu).

Choose a font from the menu at the top of the palette, then scroll to locate the character you need. If the glyphs are too small for easy identification, click the zoom buttons at the right. When you locate the glyph you want, double-click to insert it at the text insertion point. A small triangle in the corner of a glyph's box indicates alternate glyphs (**Figure 5.25**). If you use certain glyphs often, open the Favorite Glyphs area at the bottom of the palette and drag glyphs into the open boxes.

FIGURE 5.25: OpenType fonts often contain alternate glyphs for various characters. Here, Minion Pro offers seven different version of the cent symbol.

Creating fractions

Combining full-size numbers with a slash, as in 1/2, yields some very ugly fractions. For a professionally typeset document, you need to use actual fractions such as ½, ¼, and ¾. To automatically format selected text as a fraction, choose Style > Type Style > Make Fraction. You can also insert common fractions from the Glyphs palette or create fractions from any numerals using a fraction font.

Applying OpenType styles

OpenType fonts may include special styles such as fractions (½) and ordinals (1st), both of which are included in the font used in this book, Proxima Nova. The styles available in OpenType fonts vary significantly from font to font. (You can identify OpenType fonts in the QuarkXPress menu by the "O" in front of the font name.)

To see which styles are available for the active font, click the OpenType menu on the Classic tab or the Character Attributes tab of the Measurements palette (**Figure 5.26**). Options in brackets are not available in that font. You can also see available OpenType options in the OpenType area of the Character Attributes dialog box (Style > Character). Note that OpenType styles work best when applied to the appropriate text only—for example, only apply Tabular Figures to numerals not to all the text in a paragraph.

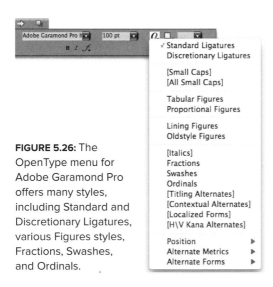

FIGURE 5.26: The OpenType menu for Adobe Garamond Pro offers many styles, including Standard and Discretionary Ligatures, various Figures styles, Fractions, Swashes, and Ordinals.

Applying ligatures

A ligature is a glyph that represents a character pair; common ligatures include "fi" and "fl" (**Figure 5.27**). For PostScript fonts, QuarkXPress can substitute "fi" and "fl" ligatures automatically when Enable Ligatures is checked in the Character tab of the Measurements palette. For OpenType fonts, you can apply the Standard Ligatures and the Discretionary Ligatures styles (if available for the font). The Glyphs palette (Window menu) displays all the ligatures available in a font.

FIGURE 5.27: Ligatures improve the readability of body text and the look of display type. Notice the difference in the word "final" in Adobe Garamond Pro Italic with ligatures disabled (left) and enabled (right).

Combining type and graphics

Interesting layouts usually feature a combination of type and graphics, including text wraps, anchored items that flow with text, rules (lines) above and below paragraphs, and text converted to boxes.

Wrapping text around items

In QuarkXPress, text can wrap around items and pictures placed in front of text. First, ensure that the item is placed in front of the text (Item > Bring to Front). Then, use the Runaround tab of the Modify dialog box (Item menu) or the Measurements palette to specify the type of runaround and how much space to leave between the item or picture and the text (**Figure 5.28**). Experiment with the various runaround options and outset values until the text wraps the way you want.

> TIP **EDITING THE RUNAROUND PATH**
>
> *To fine-tune the runaround path with the Bézier Pen tool, choose Item > Edit > Runaround to display the path.*

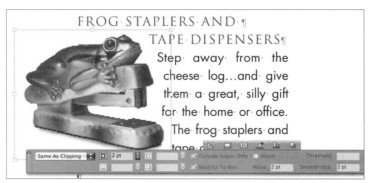

FIGURE 5.28: In this example, the text is wrapping around the picture's clipping path with an outset of 2 points.

Anchoring items in text

Anchored items flow with text just like other characters. To anchor an item, select it with the Item tool and choose Edit > Cut. Then, click the Text Content tool in text and choose Edit > Paste. When an anchored item is selected with the Item tool, the Align With Text Ascent and Align With Text Baseline buttons on the Classic tab of the Measurements palette let you position it. You can select anchored items with the Text Content tool $\boxed{T}$ just like other characters.

Applying rules to paragraphs

Although you can anchor lines in text, it's easier to place rules above or below paragraphs with the Rules tab of the Paragraph Attributes dialog box (Style > Rules). You can specify the length, width, placement, style, and color of rules for selected paragraphs and through a paragraph style sheet.

Converting text to boxes

To convert text to a box—which can then contain text or a picture—select text and choose Item > Convert Text To Boxes > Unanchored or Anchored (**Figure 5.29**).

FIGURE 5.29: After text is converted to a box, you can split the box into individual characters using Item > Split > Outside Paths.

CHAPTER 6

Tables

NOTHING HELPS YOU ORGANIZE INFORMATION LIKE A TABLE. Whether you're working with numbers in an annual report, combining pictures and text for a catalog, or just arranging pictures, QuarkXPress tables make the process easy. First, you can enter table information directly into QuarkXPress, convert text to tables, and work with Microsoft Excel files. Once the information is in a table, you have precise control over its placement and background along with row, column, cell, and gridline formatting.

As tables are adjusted, you can add and remove rows and columns, combine cells, continue tables across pages, and specify automatic headers and footers. Tables are flexible items that can be converted to grouped items and converted back to text as necessary. All the standard QuarkXPress item and content formatting options are available to tables.

In this chapter you'll learn how to create tables, work with Excel data, add content to tables, edit and format table text, format tables themselves, position tables on the page, continue tables across pages with headers and footers, and more.

Creating tables

QuarkXPress provides a variety of methods for creating tables. In some cases, you won't need an "official" QuarkXPress table at all—you might design your own table with tabs, rules above and below paragraphs, and lines. You will find, however, that these "fake" tables are difficult to adjust as the information and design changes. A QuarkXPress table is much more flexible. The method you choose for creating a table depends on the source of the table information.

- **Create a new table:** If you're entering information from hard copy, flowing text through linked cells, or importing pictures into cells, create a new table with the Table tool.

- **Convert text to a table:** If the table consists of text that is already delimited (divided by tabs and paragraph returns, for example), you can convert the text to a table.

- **Import or paste from Excel:** If the information exists in an Excel table or chart, you'll need to decide whether to import it into a new table, copy and paste the information, or import a chart.

Creating a new table

If you need to enter information into a table in QuarkXPress—including entering text in individual cells, flowing text through linked cells, and importing pictures— create a new table. Note that if text is delimited in some way (with tabs indicating columns, for example), a better option is to import the text into a text box, then convert it to a table. To create a table:

1. Select the Table tool ▦ on the Tools palette. You can press G to select it (unless the Text Content tool is selected).

2. Click and drag to draw a rectangle that is roughly the size of the final table; press Shift to constrain the rectangle to a square.

3. Release the mouse button to display the Table Properties dialog box and set up the table (**Figure 6.1**).

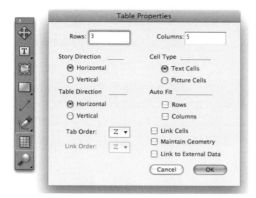

FIGURE 6.1: Use the Table Properties dialog box to specify the number of rows, number of columns, cell type, and more.

4. Enter the initial number of rows and columns based on your table data. You can add and remove rows and columns later as necessary.

5. Click OK to create the table. QuarkXPress calculates the row and column sizes according to the size of the table.

The remaining options in the Table Properties dialog box rarely need to be changed. If you need to change them, they work as follows:

- Story Direction controls whether text flows horizontally across the cell or vertically down it. For English text, this is generally set to Horizontal.

- Cell Type lets you create text cells or picture cells. Since cells can contain either text or pictures just like boxes, this setting doesn't matter much. The only difference is that if you click Picture Cells, you cannot link the cells.

- Table Direction, Tab Order, and Link Order all control how you jump from text cell to text cell (when you press Control+Tab) and how text flows through linked text cells.

- Auto Fit lets you create text cells that expand as you add text. Check Rows to increase row height to accommodate text; check Columns to increase cell width. When both are checked, maximum values specified in the Cell pane of the Modify dialog box (Item menu) control how much the cells can expand. (When Maintain Geometry is checked, the Auto Fit controls are disabled.)

- Check Link Cells to link all the text cells so imported text flows through them. (Again, if text is already delimited, it's better to convert the text to a table.) You can also link individual cells later with the Text Linking tool.

- Check Maintain Geometry to keep the size of the table consistent when the number of rows and columns changes. When this is checked, the row height and column width adjust rather than the table size.

- To import an Excel spreadsheet, check Link to External Data. This disables the Rows and Columns fields, as those will be determined by the data in Excel.

TIP **MODIFYING TABLE TOOL PREFERENCES**

You can change all the default settings for creating and formatting a table by modifying preferences for the Table tool. Double-click the Table tool to open the Tools tab of the Preferences dialog box. Select the Table tool and click Modify.

Converting text to tables

You can convert text that contains delimiters—invisible characters that indicate the difference between rows and columns—into a QuarkXPress table. Generally, the delimiters consist of tab characters between columns and paragraph returns between rows, since that is how information is often entered into Microsoft Word (**Figure 6.2**). In fact, if you import a Word table into a QuarkXPress text box, the text is imported with tab and paragraph return delimiters. The keys to successfully converting text to a table are first identifying the delimiter characters and then ensuring that they are used consistently.

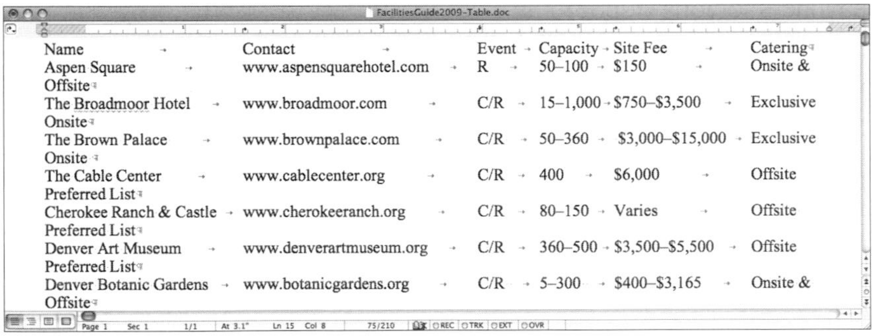

FIGURE 6.2: Delimited text prepared in Microsoft Word shows a paragraph return at the end of each row and only one tab character between each column.

To convert text to a table:

1. Import or type the text into a text box.

2. Choose View > Invisibles to display the delimiters and determine how the information is currently separated. If necessary, remove any extra characters (such as two tabs rather than one) and add any missing ones.

3. Using the Text Content tool 🅣, select the text to convert to a table.

4. Choose Table > Convert Text to Table. Confirm the settings in the Convert Text to Table dialog box (**Figure 6.3**) and click OK.

FIGURE 6.3: The Convert Text to Table dialog box is where you can control how data is divided into rows and columns, the order in which cells are filled, and whether you want to automatically fit the rows and columns to the text.

5. The new table is placed on top of the text box containing the original text (**Figure 6.4**). If you converted all the text in the box, you can delete the source text box.

Name	Contact	Event	Capacity	Site Fee	Catering
Aspen Square	www.aspen-squarehotel.com	R	50–100	$150	Onsite & Offsite
The Broadmoor Hotel	www.broadmoor.com	C/R	15–1,000	$750–$3,500	Exclusive Onsite
The Brown Palace	www.brownpalace.com	C/R	50–360	$3,000–$15,000	Exclusive Onsite
The Cable Center	www.cablecenter.org	C/R	400	$6,000	Offsite Preferred List
Cherokee Ranch & Castle	www.cherokeeranch.org	C/R	80–150	Varies	Offsite Preferred List
Denver Art Museum	www.denverartmuseum.org	C/R	360–500	$3,500–$5,500	Offsite Preferred List
Denver Botanic Gardens	www.botanicgardens.org	C/R	5–300	$400–$3,165	Onsite & Offsite

FIGURE 6.4: The delimited text in Figure 6.2 was converted to this table.

The options in the Convert Text to Table dialog box work as follows:

- The Separate Rows With and Separate Columns With menus indicate the delimiters used in the text.

- The Rows and Columns values indicate the number of rows and columns needed to contain the selected text. You can increase these values to add placeholder rows and columns. Note that if the Rows and Columns numbers look way off, you may need to click Cancel and check the delimiters in the selected text again.

- The Cell Fill Order controls the order in which the text fills the table cells. The default (left to right, from the top down) is appropriate for most U.S. English text. You might choose another option for a different language or if you want to display information in a different order (for example, list prices from lowest to highest rather than highest to lowest).

- When you convert text to a table, the rows and columns are automatically sized to contain all the selected text. The Auto Fit controls let you specify that row and column sizes continue to expand as necessary to contain text as it is edited and formatted.

Importing Excel tables and charts

You have three options for working with information from Microsoft Excel: Copy and paste delimited data, link to a spreadsheet, or import a chart as a picture.

- **Copy and paste:** QuarkXPress can quickly create a table for you based on information copied from an Excel spreadsheet. The table data, however, is not linked to the Excel spreadsheet and will not update. To do this, copy rows and columns from a spreadsheet in Excel. Switch to QuarkXPress, and paste the information into a text box. A table is created automatically.

- **Link to Excel:** You can link a newly created table to an Excel spreadsheet, then update the table as the data in Excel changes (through Utilities > Usage > Tables). When you update table data, however, text formatting applied in QuarkXPress is not maintained and other adjustments may occur. To link to a spreadsheet, create a table with the Table tool, then check Link to External Data in the Table Properties dialog box. Browse to the spreadsheet, select the sheet you want to import, and set the import options (**Figure 6.5**).

FIGURE 6.5: Use the Table Link dialog box to select a sheet of a spreadsheet to import.

- **Importing charts:** Charts inserted into Excel (through Insert > Chart or Insert > Picture) can be imported into QuarkXPress as pictures. The disadvantage to this method is that most graphic designers prefer more sophisticated chart designs than those used for utilitarian spreadsheet purposes. To import a chart, choose File > Import, select the Excel file, and use the Chart pane to select the chart to import. If the chart changes, you can update through Utilities > Usage > Pictures.

Working with tables

Understanding the components of a QuarkXPress table will help you remember which tools to use while working with them. A table is an item—so you make adjustments to its size, placement, background, and frame by selecting it with the Item tool ⊕. The rows, columns, and cells in a table, however, are all treated as contents—so you make adjustments with commands in the Table menu, the Text Content tool 🄣, or the Picture Content tool 🖻. Table cells are essentially mini boxes that can contain text boxes or pictures.

Adding text and pictures

Table cells are essentially boxes that can contain text or a picture. To add contents to empty cells, you can type text into them, paste text or pictures into them, or import text or pictures through File > Import or drag and drop from the desktop. A few notes about adding text:

- When typing text into table cells, press Control+Tab to jump to the next cell or Control+Shift+Tab to jump to the previous cell.

- You can import text into an individual cell or a series of linked cells. You can specify linked cells in the Table Properties dialog box when you create a new table or you can link individual cells using the Text Linking tool.

- When working with linked cells, use the Next Column character (Enter on the keypad) to force text to the next linked cell.

If you are working with delimited text—such as tabular data—use Table > Convert Text to Table rather than manually adding all the text to table cells.

Editing and formatting table text

To edit and format table text, always use the Text Content tool $\boxed{\text{T}}$. In general, you make text selections, edit text, and format text the same way you do when working with text in boxes. In addition, you can position text within cells and link text cells as if you were working with text boxes.

Editing text

When working with text in table cells, select it; cut, copy, and paste it; and navigate through it with the arrow keys as you do when working with text in boxes. When working with table text:

- Press the arrow keys on the keyboard to move the text insertion point within cells and from cell to cell.

- Click and drag the Text Content tool to select text in multiple, adjacent cells.

- Click the edges of a table with the Text Content tool to select all the text in a row or column (**Figure 6.6**). Click and drag to select multiple rows or columns; Shift+click to select noncontinuous rows or columns. Note that the table must already be selected.

FIGURE 6.6: Click the Text Content tool outside a table to select rows and columns.

- Choose options from the Select submenu of the Table menu to make other helpful text selections: Cell, Row, Odd Rows, Even Rows, Column, Odd Columns, Even Columns, All Cells, Header Rows, Footer Rows, and Body Rows.

TIP *ALIGNING TABLE DATA ON DECIMAL POINTS*

When working with dollar values, you may need to align data within cells on decimal points. To do this, you need to type a tab before each value, then align the tab stops on the decimal point (Style > Tabs > Align On).

Applying paragraph and character attributes

When text in table cells is selected, you can format it the same way you format any other text—using options in the Style menu, the Measurements palette, and the Style Sheets palette (**Figure 6.7**).

FIGURE 6.7: In this example, the Table Copy paragraph style sheet is applied to the body text in the rows. The Facility Name character style sheet, which specifies a bold font, will be applied to the names in the first column.

Positioning text within table cells

To precisely position text within selected table cells, you can specify all the same options that are available for text boxes. These include text inset and vertical alignment, one of which you will probably need to change to prevent the text from touching the cell's gridlines (**Figure 6.8**). You might change the angle of text within a cell to create vertical row labels. The Text pane of the Measurements palette and Modify dialog box (Item menu) provide controls for positioning text within table cells (**Figure 6.9**). For consistent positioning, be sure to select all the cells in a table.

NAME	CONTACT	EVENT	CAPACITY	SITE FEE	CATERING
ASPEN SQUARE	www.aspensquarehotel.com	R	50–100	$150	Onsite & Offsite
THE BROADMOOR HOTEL	www.broadmoor.com	C/R	15–1,000	$750–$3,500	Exclusive-Onsite
THE BROWN PALACE	www.brownpalace.com	C/R	50–360	$3,000–$15,000	Exclusive-Onsite
THE CABLE CENTER	www.cablecenter.org	C/R	400	$6,000	Offsite Preferred List
CHEROKEE RANCH & CASTLE	www.cherokeeranch.org	C/R	80–150	Varies	Offsite Preferred List
DENVER ART MUSEUM	www.denverartmuseum.org	C/R	360–500	$3,500–$5,500	Offsite Preferred List
DENVER BOTANIC GARDENS	www.botanicgardens.org	C/R	5–300	$400–$3,165	Onsite & Offsite

FIGURE 6.8: In this example, text is inset from the edges of the cells and the horizontal gridlines have a width of zero (and therefore do not display).

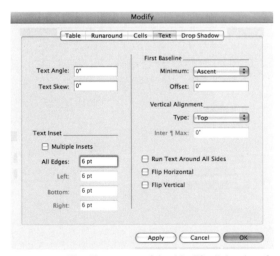

FIGURE 6.9: The Text pane of the Modify dialog box for tables (Item menu) is similar to the Text pane for text boxes.

Linking table cells

You can link table cells so text flows through them—although you are not likely to do this often as the data in a cell is often self-contained. To link cells:

- Use the Text Linking tool and Text Unlinking tool to create and break links (respectively) between text cells in a table.

- Check Link Cells in the Table Properties dialog box when you create the table; this links all the cells in the table.

- Choose Table > Link Text Cells to link selected cells in a table. As with linking text boxes, only the first cell can contain text when you link cells. That text will flow through the linked cells.

Formatting tables

Table formats come in three flavors—formats that apply to the entire table such as its frame and background, formats that apply to all or selected gridlines, and formats that apply to all or selected cells. By combining all these formats along with paragraph and character attributes, you can create an attractive, easy-to-read table. To format an entire table, select it with the Item tool ⊕. To format gridlines, rows, columns, and cells, select them with the Text Content tool Ⓣ.

Framing tables

To place a frame (otherwise known as a stroke) outside the edges of a table, select the table with the Item tool. You can then use the Frame tab of the Measurements palette or Modify dialog box (Item menu) to specify the width, style, and color of the frame (**Figure 6.10**).

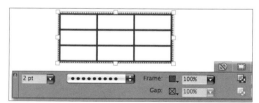

FIGURE 6.10: When a table is selected with the Item tool, you can use the Frame tab of the Measurements palette to modify its frame.

Creating table backgrounds

A table can have a single background color, blend, or picture. In order for the background to display, the table's cells need to have a transparent background.

- **Background color:** To specify a background color for a table, first select all the cells and make sure they have a transparent background (Item > Modify > Cells > Opacity > [less than 100%]). Then, select the table with the Item tool and specify the color, shade, and opacity in the Table tab of the Measurements palette or Modify dialog box (Item menu).

- **Background picture:** To use a picture for a table background, place the table on top of the picture. Then, be sure the table background *and* the table cells are transparent (Item > Modify > Table/Cells tab > Opacity > [less than 100%]).

Formatting gridlines

The lines between rows and columns are called gridlines, and they can be formatted with a specified width, style, and color like any other line in QuarkXPress. To select gridlines for formatting:

- Click the Text Content tool ⊞ to select a single gridline; Shift+click to select multiple gridlines.

- Choose an option from the Table > Select submenu: Horizontal Grids, Vertical Grids, Border, or All Grids.

- Select the table with the Item tool, then click the selection buttons in the Grid tab of the Modify dialog box (Item menu): Select All, Select Vertical, or Select Horizontal.

Once gridlines are selected, you can make changes to them in the Table Grid tab of the Measurements palette or the Grid tab of the Modify dialog box (Item menu). See Figures 6.11–6.12.

FIGURE 6.11: The Table Grid tab of the Measurements palette is available when gridlines are selected. You can choose the line width, style, and color.

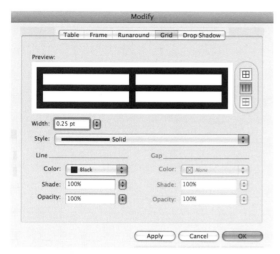

FIGURE 6.12: The three buttons in the upper-right corner of the Grid tab let you select table gridlines for formatting.

Formatting cells, rows, and columns

You can format cells—and entire rows and columns of cells—with the same background color, shade, opacity, and blend options as boxes. For readability, every other row or every other column of a table is often formatted differently. The key to formatting cells is selecting them:

- **Individual cell:** Click the Text Content tool 𝕋 to select a cell.

- **All cells:** Click in a table and choose Table > Select > All Cells.

- **Individual row or column:** Click the Text Content tool outside a selected table. Or click in a cell and choose Table > Select > Row or Table > Select > Column.

- **Adjacent rows or columns:** Drag the Text Content tool along the edge of a selected table.

- **Noncontinuous rows or columns:** Shift+click the Text Content tool along the edge of a selected table.

- **Pattern of rows or columns:** Choose Table > Select > Odd Rows, Even Rows, Odd Columns, or Even Columns. If you're working with header rows and footer rows in a continued table, you can also choose Header Rows, Footer Rows, or Body Rows (**Figure 6.13**).

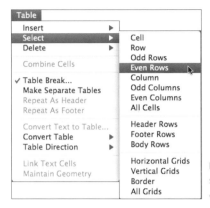

FIGURE 6.13: The Table > Select submenu lets you select a pattern of rows or columns for formatting.

Once cells are selected, you can change the background in the Classic tab of the Measurements palette or the Cells tab of the Modify dialog box (Item menu). See Figure 6.14.

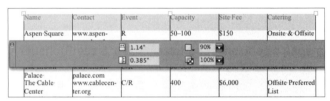

FIGURE 6.14: Use the Classic tab of the Measurements palette to select a color, shade, and opacity for the background of selected cells.

Positioning tables on the page

You can place a table anywhere you want on the page the same way you position other items. Select the table with the Item tool ⊕ and drag it, enter X and Y values in the Classic tab of the Measurements palette, or enter Origin Across and Origin Down values in the Table tab of the Modify dialog box (Item menu). You can also rotate the table using the Item tool or by entering a value in an Angle field (Figure 6.15).

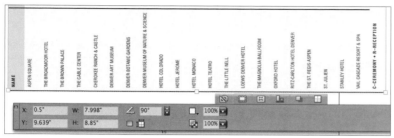

FIGURE 6.15: This table was rotated by entering 90° in the Angle field of the Classic tab of the Measurements palette.

Adjusting tables

As information changes, you may need to make adjustments to a table such as changing its size, adding or removing rows or columns, and merging cells. You can do all these things plus precisely control column width and row height.

Inserting rows or columns

You can insert a row above or below the selected row, and you can insert a column to the left or right of the selected column. To select a row or column, click in a cell with the Text Content tool 𝕋. Then, choose Table > Insert > Row or Table > Insert > Column. Specify the number of rows or columns to insert and the location (Figure 6.16). You can check Keep Attributes to insert rows or columns with the same background and gridline formatting as the selected row or column.

FIGURE 6.16: Use the Insert Table Rows dialog box to specify the number of rows to insert, the location, and the formatting.

Deleting rows or columns

If you no longer need certain rows or columns, you can delete them. First, select the rows or columns to delete using the Text Content tool $\boxed{\text{T}}$ or the Table > Select submenu. Then, choose Table > Delete > Row or Table > Delete > Column. Table contents are deleted as well—except for text that is able to flow into other linked text cells.

Merging and splitting cells

Cells can be merged and split as necessary to fit your content. You might, for example, merge the cells in a table's first row to create a heading that spans the table. To select the cells to merge, Shift+click a rectangular area of adjacent cells with the Text Content tool $\boxed{\text{T}}$. Then, choose Table > Combine Cells (**Figure 6.17**). To restore combined cells to their previous configuration, select a combined cell and choose Table > Split Cells.

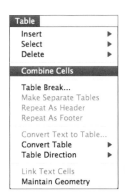

FIGURE 6.17: Choose Table > Combine Cells to merge selected table cells.

Fixing table dimensions

If you prefer fixed table dimensions—that is, you don't want the dimensions of a table to change when you adjust the number of rows and columns—check Maintain Geometry in the Table menu. You can also check Maintain Geometry in the Table Properties dialog box when you create a table and in the Table tab of the Modify dialog box (Item menu). It's easier to understand Maintain Geometry in an example: If you add a row to a table for which Maintain Geometry is checked, the height of the other rows is reduced to squeeze in another row; if you add a row in a table for which Maintain Geometry is *unchecked,* the height of the entire table is increased.

Adjusting rows and columns to fit text

If you're typing text into table cells, you can use the Auto Fit feature to specify that cells automatically expand to fit all the text. Auto Fit also works when you increase the font size of text in cells. The Auto Fit feature, however, does not work in the opposite direction—cells do not decrease in size as text is deleted or resized. In addition, when you're working with linked cells, text that doesn't fit into one cell simply flows into the next cell.

Enable Auto Fit for selected rows or columns in the Cells tab of the Modify dialog box (Item menu) shown in **Figure 6.18.**

- If you want the cell width to expand, check Auto Fit under Column Width and specify a maximum width.

- If you want the cell height to expand, check Auto Fit under Row Height and specify a maximum height.

- If you enable Auto Fit for both columns and rows, column width expands first.

- Once cells expand to its maximum size, text overflows.

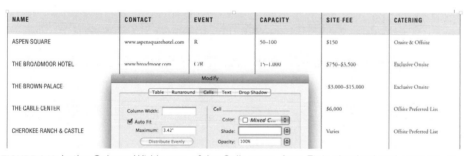

FIGURE 6.18: In the Column Width area of the Cells pane, Auto Fit is checked and a maximum width of 1.42" is specified.

TIP *MAINTAIN GEOMETRY VS. AUTO FIT*

Maintain Geometry (Table menu) and Auto Fit are mutually exclusive features—you can either fix the table dimensions or you can specify that rows, columns, or both automatically expand to accommodate text.

Resizing tables, rows, and columns

You can resize tables, rows, and columns by entering specific height and width values into fields and by dragging the table or gridlines with the mouse.

- **Resize a selected table:** Enter values in the Width and Height fields in the Table pane of the Modify dialog box (Item menu) or Classic tab of the Measurements palette.

- **Resize selected rows and columns:** Enter values in the Column Width and Row Height fields in the Cells pane of the Modify dialog box (Item menu).

- **Distribute selected rows or columns evenly:** To create rows or columns of equal size that fit within the selected area, click Distribute Evenly under Column Width or Row Height in the Cells pane of the Modify dialog box.

Using the Text Content tool [T], you can drag gridlines to resize rows and columns (Figure 6.19). Using the Item tool [✛], you can drag a table handle to resize the table.

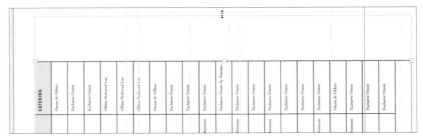

FIGURE 6.19: Using the Text Content tool, drag a gridline to resize a column.

TIP **RESIZING TABLE ELEMENTS**

When you resize a table with the Item tool, you can press Command (Mac) or Control (Windows) to resize the rows and columns along with the table. Add the Shift key to resize the table, rows, and columns while constraining the shape to a square. To resize the table, rows, and columns proportionally, press Command+Option+Shift (Mac) or Control+Alt+Shift (Windows) as you resize the table.

Continuing tables across pages

Tables are not expected to always fit on a single page—or even within a defined space on one page. You can "break" a table and then continue it in another location, which is generally on another page but can be on the same page. After you break a table, you can add automatic header and footer rows to help identify the table contents.

Breaking a table

To continue a table in another location, you have to "break" it into segments. Unfortunately, you don't get to choose when and where the table breaks. Instead, in a nonintuitive process, QuarkXPress breaks the table for you when it gets "too big." (You do get to define what "too big" means.) If the table gets too small, the table segments are automatically recombined. To break a table:

1. Select the table and choose Table > Table Break.

2. To break the table when it reaches a maximum width, check Width. Enter the maximum width the table can reach before it splits between columns.

3. To break the table when it reaches a maximum height, check Height. Enter the maximum height the table can reach before it splits between rows.

4. To split the table right away, decrease the value in the Width or Height field.

Note that if you leave the maximum Width or Height value at the default setting, which is the current table width and height of the table, nothing happens until you expand the table beyond these values. In general, check Width *or* Height as table break criteria—not both.

When the table breaks, it splits into two or more linked table segments. You can move the table segments to other locations in the layout (**Figure 6.20**). Any changes to the table, such as inserted rows or columns, are reflected throughout all the table segments.

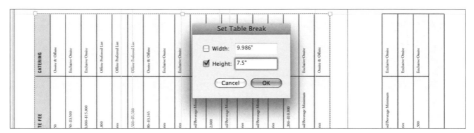

FIGURE 6.20: In this example, the rotated table exceeded its maximum height. A continued instance of the table was moved to the next page.

> TIP **SEPARATING TABLE SEGMENTS**
>
> *You can convert the segments of a broken table into individual tables. To do this, select any segment of the table and choose Table > Make Separate Tables. The resulting tables are no longer linked, so changes to one table will not affect the other tables.*

Adding header and footer rows

The first row of a table usually contains labels for the columns so you know what's in them. The last row of a table often provides other useful information. You can automatically repeat and update this information by specifying these rows as official "header" and "footer" rows for a table. You can only specify header and footer rows for a table that has already split because it reached the maximum height specified in the Table Break dialog box.

- To specify header rows for a table, select the first row (or several rows) and choose Table > Repeat as Header (**Figure 6.21**).

- To specify footer rows for a table, select the last row (or several rows) and choose Table > Repeat as Footer.

Insert	▶
Select	▶
Delete	▶
Combine Cells	
✓ Table Break...	
Make Separate Tables	
Repeat As Header	
Repeat As Footer	
Convert Text to Table...	
Convert Table	▶
Table Direction	▶
Link Text Cells	
Maintain Geometry	

FIGURE 6.21: Choose Table > Repeat as Header to specify that selected rows are header rows.

- The header and footer rows are added to all the table segments, increasing their height and possibly resulting in additional table segments (**Figure 6.22**).

- Text in all header and footer rows is automatically synchronized. This means you cannot add words such as "continued from page 1" to the header on the second segment of a table on page 2.

NAME	CONTACT	EVENT
ASPEN SQUARE	www.aspensquarehotel.com	R
THE BROADMOOR HOTEL	www.broadmoor.com	C/R
THE BROWN PALACE	www.brownpalace.com	C/R
THE CABLE CENTER	www.cablecenter.org	C/R
LOEWS DENVER HOTEL	www.loewshotels.com	C/R
THE MAGNOLIA BALLROOM	www.magnoliahoteldenver.com	R
OXFORD HOTEL	www.theoxfordhotel.com	C/R
RITZ-CARLTON HOTEL DENVER	www.ritzcarlton.com	C/R
C–CEREMONY • R–RECEPTION		

NAME	CONTACT	EVENT
THE ST. REGIS ASPEN	www.stregisaspen.com	C/R
ST. JULIEN	www.stjulien.com	C/R
STANLEY HOTEL	www.stanleyhotel.com	C/R
VAIL CASCADE RESORT & SPA	www.vailcascade.com	C/R
C–CEREMONY • R–RECEPTION		

FIGURE 6.22: In these table segments, the header row labels the columns while the footer row provides a key to the information.

Exporting table data

Information in a QuarkXPress table is not stuck there—you can export it as delimited text. The table data is copied out of the cells and placed in a new text box; picture cells are converted to anchored boxes within the text. When you export table data, you will need to decide what order to extract the table data in, the delimit characters (such as tabs and paragraph returns) you want to separate the row and column information with, and whether to delete the source table. To export table data, select the table and choose Table > Convert Table > To Text.

Converting tables to groups

If you want to take apart a table—for example, break up the cells and use them as individual sidebars rather than as a table—you can convert a table to a group. When you do this, each cell becomes an individual text box or a picture box (containing its table contents). To convert a table to a group, choose Table > Convert Table > To Group. (If you still need parts of the table, convert a copy of the table to a group by first choosing Item > Duplicate.) To separate the boxes in the group, choose Item > Ungroup.

CHAPTER 7

Pictures

THE ABILITY TO IMPORT AND MANIPULATE GRAPHICS—photos, illustrations, charts, and such—has been a hallmark of page layout software since the dawn of desktop publishing in the 1980s. In addition to standard image-manipulation features like crop and scale, QuarkXPress 8 also includes many features that were once available only in image-editing software—features like unsharp masking (edge sharpening), brightness and contrast adjustment, and tonal adjustment. The ability to perform many basic image-editing tasks within QuarkXPress can save you time and simplify your workflow

In this chapter you'll learn how to import graphics—or pictures as they're called in QuarkXPress—into your layouts and how to make basic changes to themlike cropping and scaling. You'll also learn to use some of the program's image-editing features to adjust the appearance of some types of imported pictures, and you'll discover how to export picture files that include adjustments you've made in QuarkXPress.

Importing

Previous versions of QuarkXPress required users to create and select a picture box before importing a picture; however, these preconditions have been removed in QuarkXPress 8. To import a picture:

1. If you want, you can create a picture box or a no-content box at the location on the page or pasteboard where you want to place the imported picture. If a picture box is not selected when you import a picture, an new picture box is created in the center of the current page.

2. Choose File > Import.

3. In the Import dialog box (**Figure 7.1**), locate and select the picture you want to import. Make sure the Preview option is checked so that you can see a preview of the picture before you import it.

4. Click Open.

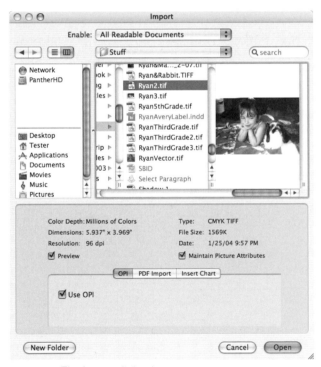

FIGURE 7.1 The Import dialog box.

If a picture box or no-content box was selected when you chose File > Import, the upper-left corner of the picture is placed in the upper-left corner of the selected box. If the box is larger than the picture's dimensions, the entire picture will be visible. If the box is smaller than the picture's dimensions, the bottom or right edge, or both, will be cropped.

After you import a picture, any cropped areas of the image are "ghosted" (displayed lighter) to distinguish these areas from the visible portion of the picture (Figure 7.2). If nothing is selected when you import a picture, the picture is placed within a new picture box that is centered on the current page and placed at the top of the stacking order.

FIGURE 7.2 If you import a picture into a box that's smaller than the dimensions of the picture, cropped areas (portions of the picture that are outside the box) are "ghosted" to distinguish them from the live portion of the picture.

TIP: **DRAGGING AND DROPPING PICTURES**

In addition to using the Import command (File menu) to import pictures, you can also drag and drop picture files from the Mac desktop, Windows Explorer, and Adobe Bridge into QuarkXPress layouts. With the drag-and-drop method you can select and import place multiple files, including a combination of text and picture files.

A word of caution about importing pictures: The Import command is available when you're in text-editing mode—that is, when the cursor is flashing or text is highlighted. If you import a picture under either of these circumstances, the new picture box is placed within the active text box as an anchored item. An anchored item is treated as a text character within the text stream. You can't use the Item tool to reposition anchored items. (For more about anchored items, see Chapter 5.)

TIP: **SUPPORTED GRAPHIC FORMATS**

QuarkXPress supports import of the following graphic file formats: native Adobe Illustrator (.AI), bitmap (.bmp), .dcs, .eps, .gif, .jpg, .pdf, .png, native Adobe Photoshop (.psd), .swf, .tif, and .wmf.

Cropping, positioning, and scaling

Before you begin to modify imported pictures, it's important to understand the difference between selecting a picture box with the Item tool and selecting a picture with the Picture Content tool ( ):

- Use the Item tool if you want to move a picture box or scale both a picture box and the picture within. When you select a picture box with the Item tool, white resizing handles are displayed at the corners of the item's bounding box and the midpoints of the edges.

- Use the Picture Content tool if you want to modify a picture—for example, by moving the picture within its box or scaling it—without affecting the picture box. When you select a picture box with the Picture Content tool, circular shapes are displayed at the corners of the picture and the midpoints of its edges and resizing handles are displayed at the corners of the item's bounding box and the midpoints of the bounding box edges. Portions of the picture that are outside the box are lightened to show you what's being clipped.

For some tasks, particularly cropping, it's possible to use either tool.

Cropping

If you want to print only part of a picture, you have the option of cropping the graphic file using an image-editing program. But an easier option—and one that doesn't actually delete anything from the original graphic file—is to crop imported pictures within QuarkXPress. Although the Item tool lets you crop pictures, the Picture Content tool is generally better for this task because you're able to see what's being cropped as you drag the mouse.

When you click a picture box with the Picture Content tool, any cropped areas of the picture are lightened to distinguish them from the live area. Click and drag any of the eight square resizing handles to crop the picture within. As you drag handles, the onscreen display is continually updated to show you what portion of the picture is inside the picture box and what areas are getting cropped. **Figure 7.3** shows a before, during, and after example of cropping.

Cropping a picture with the Picture Content tool gets a little tricky when the small, square resizing handles of a picture box overlap the rounded blue resizing handles of a picture. When this occurs, clicking a box's resizing handle will actually select the picture resizing handle, and if you drag, you'll change the scale of the picture. The trick here is to first press the Command key (Mac) or Control key (Windows), click a box resizing handle, release the Command or Control key, and then drag. If you don't release the Command or Control key before you drag, you'll scale both the picture and the box. Unfortunately, when you use a modifier key, only the portion of the picture within the box is visible as you drag.

FIGURE 7.3 The picture on the left is selected with the Picture Content tool. The square resizing handles of the picture box coincide with the rounded resizing handles of the picture, indicating that the dimensions of the picture box are the same as the dimensions of the picture. Middle: After using the Item tool to drag the picture box's resizing handles and then selecting the picture with the Picture Content tool, the cropped areas are visible beyond the edge of the picture box. Right: The final, cropped picture selected with the Item tool.

Positioning a picture within its box

If you want to move a picture box—and the picture within—simply click and drag the box with the Item tool (Chapter 3 explains how to move items); however, if you want to move a picture within its box, use the Picture Content tool. When this tool is selected and you move the pointer over a picture box that contains a picture, the hand pointer ( ) is displayed. Click and drag when this pointer appears to move the picture. Press the Shift key as you drag to constrain movement to vertical and horizontal. A live preview is displayed as you drag, with cropped areas lightened.

The arrow keys offer a useful alternative to moving a picture with the mouse. When you select a picture with the Picture Content tool, each click of an arrow key nudges the picture one point. Hold down the Option key (Mac) or the Alt key (Windows) to reduce the nudge increment to one-tenth of a point.

If you're fond of using the Measurements palette to make changes to items, you can click the increase/decrease arrows next to the Offset Across (X+) and Offset Down (Y+) fields in the Classic tab to move a selected picture in one-point increments. Hold down the Option key (Mac) or the Alt key (Windows) to reduce the nudge increment to one-tenth of a point. Figure 7.4 shows the Offset Across and Offset Down controls in the Measurements palette. Of course, you can also specify offset values in the fields. If you want to place the upper-left corner of the picture in the upper-left corner of the box (the default position), enter 0 in these fields, which are also available in the Picture pane of the Modify dialog box (Item > Modify).

FIGURE 7.4 Clicking the Offset Across Increase button moves the selected picture one point to the right.

Scaling pictures

As with cropping, you have several options for scaling pictures. The quickest and easiest way to scale both a picture box and the picture within is to select the box with the Item tool, and then drag a resizing handle while holding down Shift+Command (Mac) or Shift+Control (Windows). Holding down the modifier keys maintains the proportions of both the picture and the box. If you hold down only the Command or Control key, you can disproportionately scale the picture and the box.

If you've selected a picture with the Picture Content tool, you can drag any of its resizing handles to scale the picture without affecting the box. Hold down Shift+Command (Mac) or Shift+Control (Windows) as you drag to maintain the proportions of the picture. If you hold down only the Command or Control key as you drag, the picture is disproportionately scaled.

The Scale Across (X%) and Scale Down (Y%) fields in the Classic tab of the Measurements palette provide another option for scaling pictures, as do the same fields in the Picture pane of the Modify dialog box (Item > Modify).

To return a picture to its original scale, set the Scale Across (X%) and Scale Down (Y%) values to 100%.

> TIP: **CONTEXT MENU COMMANDS FOR SCALING PICTURES AND RESIZING PICTURE BOXES**
>
> *If you Control+click (Mac) or right-click (Windows) a picture box with either the Item tool or the Picture Content tool, the context menu offers two commands for picture boxes. Choose Scale Picture to Box to resize the picture so that it fits completely within the box (that is, with no cropping) while maintaining the picture's original proportions. (If the dimensions of the picture are not proportional with the dimensions of the box, the box background will be visible between the edge of the picture and the top and bottom edges or left and right edges of the picture box.) Choose Fit Box to Picture to resize a picture box so that its edges align with the edges of the picture.*

More options for working with pictures

Cropping and scaling are probably the two most common changes you'll make to pictures, but other options—like rotation, skew, and opacity—let you make more dramatic changes. Nearly all of the controls for modifying pictures are available in the Picture pane of the Modify dialog box (**Figure 7.5**). Most of these controls are also available in the Classic tab of the Measurements palette (**Figure 7.6**).

Here's a quick description of the options:

- **Offset Across/Offset Down:** Move a picture within its frame.

- **Scale Across/Scale Down:** Scale a picture horizontally and vertically.

- **Picture Angle:** Rotate a picture (but not a picture box).

- **Skew:** Slant a picture so that it tilts to the left (negative values) or right (positive values).

- **Picture:** The controls in this section let you apply color, shade, and opacity to black-and-white and grayscale pictures.

- **Picture Background:** The controls in this section let you apply color, shade, and opacity to the background of black-and-white and grayscale pictures.

- **Flip Horizontal/Flip Vertical:** Lets you create a mirror image of a picture along a horizontal or vertical axis.

- **Suppress Printout:** Prevents a picture (but not a frame, if the picture box has one) from printing. Choosing this option can reduce print time and save ink if you don't need to include a particular picture.

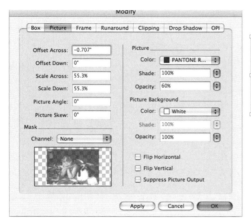

FIGURE 7.5 Modify dialog box: Picture pane.

FIGURE 7.6 Measurements pane: Classic tab. The six controls at the left of the palette let you modify a picture box; the remaining controls let you modify the picture within.

Working with Photoshop files

Early versions of QuarkXPress did not include image-editing features, such as the ability to show and hide layers, adjust color levels and contrast, and sharpen edges. A separate program was needed for this kind of work. Not any more. With QuarkXPress 8 you can import native Photoshop (.psd) files and use the PSD Import palette (Window > PSD Import) to manipulate layers, channels, and paths; and you can use the Picture Effects palette (Window > Picture Effects) to perform many common image-editing tasks.

Importing

Importing a Photoshop file is the same as importing any other type of graphic file. You can either choose File > Import or you can drag and drop one or more .psd files from the Mac desktop, Windows Explorer, or Adobe Bridge into a QuarkXPress project. A couple of things to note about QuarkXPress's support of Photoshop files:

- Layer information in some Photoshop files, including pictures that include layer effects (for example, a blending mode or a drop shadow), is not recognized. QuarkXPress uses a composite image for such pictures and you cannot adjust layers.

- You cannot use the Picture Effects palette (which is explained in the next section of this chapter) to modify imported Photoshop files.

Adjusting layers, channels, and paths

When a native Photoshop picture is selected (you can use either the Item tool or the Picture Content tool to select), the controls in the three panes of the PSD Import palette let you manipulate the picture's layers, channels, and paths. If you're familiar with Photoshop, you'll be immediately comfortable using the PSD Import palette, but even if you're not a Photoshop user, the interface is intuitive and easy to use. Here's a description of the controls that are available in each pane:

- **Layers:** This pane displays a list of a picture's layers. All pictures have at least one layer; some have more. Click the box to the left of a layer to alternately show and hide the layer. An eye in the box (👁) indicates that the layer is visible. When you select a layer, the choice you make from the Blend Mode menu at the top-left of the pane determines how the layer interacts with any layers that are beneath it. The default blend mode (Normal) makes a layer opaque. You can reduce the value in the Opacity field (to the right of the Blend Mode menu) to make a layer translucent. The lower the opacity, the lighter and more translucent the layer. **Figure 7.7** shows a before-and-after example of adjusting layer visibility and opacity.

FIGURE 7.7 PSD Import Palette: Layers pane. The picture on the left is the original, unmodified Photoshop file. The picture on the right shows the result of hiding the Text Layer and reducing the opacity of the Backdrop layer from 100% to 40%.

- **Channels:** This pane displays a list of a picture's channels. Click the box to the left of a channel to alternately show and hide the channel. Black-and-white, grayscale, and indexed color pictures have one channel; RGB pictures have three channels (red, green, and blue); and CMYK pictures have four channels (cyan, magenta, yellow, and black). You can also add channels to a Photoshop picture for such things as varnishes and embossing. **Figure 7.8** shows a before-and-after example of adjusting the visibility of channels.

FIGURE 7.8 PSD Import Palette: Channels pane. The picture on the left is the original, unmodified Photoshop file. The picture on the right shows the result of using a channel to apply a varnish to the silhouetted area of the picture. (The opacity of the Backdrop layer was also reduced from 100% to 40%.)

- Paths: This pane displays a list of the paths embedded within a picture, if it has any. Two boxes are displayed to the left of each path name. The boxes in the left column let you select the path that's used to wrap text around the picture. Click an empty box to select the path to use for wrapping text. When a path is selected, this icon is displayed: ⊞. (You don't have to select a path for text wrap, and you can select only one at a time.) Click a selected box to deselect it

  The boxes in the right column let you choose a path to use a clipping path that reveals only a portion of the image. When a path is selected, this icon is displayed: ⊡. (You don't have to select a clipping path, and you can select only one at a time.) Click a selected box to deselect it. **Figure 7.9** shows an example of using a path as a clipping path and to wrap text.

Perspicax matrimonii deciperet pretosius agricolae. Ossifragi amputat utilitas suis,

Text Layer

etiam apparatus bellissimo celeriter circumgrediet quadrupei, utcunque agricolae ⊠

Perspicax matrimonii deciperet pretosius agricolae. Ossifragi amputat utilitas suis, etiam apparatus bellissimo celeriter circumgrediet quadrupei, utcunque agricolae adquireret tremulus zothecas. Satis perspicax ruresser decipe rettin agricolae, quodray lascivius chirographi suffragarit gulosus concubine, etPretosius matrimonii pessimus lucide vocificat verecun-⊠

Text Layer

FIGURE 7.9 PSD Import Palette: Paths pane. The picture on the left is the original, unmodified Photoshop file. Notice that the text wraps around the picture box. The picture on the right shows the result of using a path for clipping the image and wrapping text.

Each of the three tabs in the PSD Import palette include a menu with commands that let you revert individual or all layers, channels, and paths to their original state.

When a Photoshop picture is selected, a small, green circle is displayed at the lower-right of the PSD Import palette to indicate that the picture file has not been moved or modified. A red stop sign with a question mark is displayed for modified and missing pictures. Clicking the stop sign updates a modified picture and displays the Picture pane of the Usage dialog box if the picture file is missing.

Special effects for pictures

The Picture Effects palette (Window > Picture Effects) provides a broad set of image-editing options that let you modify the appearance of imported bitmap pictures (though not vector graphics). Common bitmap formats include .tif, .jpg, .png, and .gif.

The changes you make to pictures using the Picture Effects palette are nondestructive. That is, your changes are saved within the project file while the original picture file remains unchanged. If you want, you can use the Save Picture command (File menu) to export modified pictures so that you have a version of the graphic file that includes the changes. (More about exporting pictures later in this chapter.)

The Picture Effects palette has two menus with commands for modifying a selected picture: the Adjustments menu ▦ and the Filters menu ▼.

Making adjustments

The 12 commands in the Adjustments menu let you change the appearance of a picture by analyzing and adjusting its pixels. For example, Brightness/Contrast lets you make a picture lighter or darker, while Threshold lets you convert a color image to black-and-white and specify the value threshold that distinguishes black from white. You can apply as many different adjustments—and filters—as you want to a single picture.

To make an adjustment to a selected bitmap picture:

1. Choose an option from the Adjustments menu.

2. Use the controls in the dialog box that's displayed to modify the appearance of the picture. Each option offers a different set of controls. Check the Preview box to display changes as you make them.

3. When you're done making changes, click OK. **Figure 7.10** shows a before-and-after example of making an adjustment to a picture.

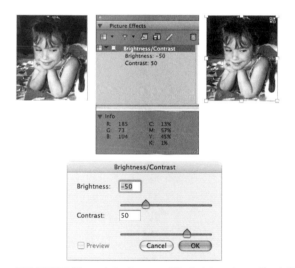

FIGURE 7.10 The original, unmodified picture is on the left. Using the Picture Effects palette to adjust the picture's Brightness/Contrast settings produced the result on the right. The Brightness/Contrast dialog box shows the applied settings.

Applying filters

The 12 commands in the Filters layer let you change the appearance of a picture based on value differences within the picture. For example, the Unsharp Mask filter increases the contrast where relatively light areas meet relatively dark areas.

To apply a filter to a selected bitmap picture:

1. Choose an option from the Filters menu.

2. Use the controls in the dialog box that's displayed to modify the appearance of the picture. Each option offers a different set of controls. Check the Preview box to display changes as you make them.

3. When you're done making changes, click OK. **Figure 7.11** shows a before-and-after example of applying a filter to a picture.

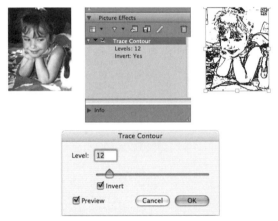

FIGURE 7.11 The original, unmodified picture is on the left. Using the Picture Effects palette to apply the Trace Contour filter produced the result on the right. The Trace Contour dialog box shows the applied settings.

Each time you make an adjustment or apply a filter to a picture, the effect is listed in the Picture Effects palette. Click the check box to the left of an effect in the list to alternately show and hide it. Click the small arrow to the left of the check box to alternately show and hide the settings for the effect. A small icon ( ) is displayed in the upper-right corner of pictures to which you've made an adjustment or applied a filter.

To remove an adjustment or filter, select it from the list in the Picture Effects palette, and then click the Delete Effect icon at the top-right of the palette ( ).

Using presets

After you've used the Picture Effects palette to make adjustments and apply filters to a picture, you can save the settings as a preset that you can use to apply the same settings to other pictures. Using presets, like paragraph and character style sheets, is a great way to save time and ensure consistency.

To save a preset, select a picture that you've modified using the Picture Effects pane, and then click the Save Preset button (🖫) at the top of the palette. Click Save in the Save Preset dialog box. By default, presets are assigned a .vpf file extension and stored within the Picture Effects Presets folder within the QuarkXPress program folder. The Picture Effects pane in the Preferences dialog box (QuarkXPress > Preferences with a Mac; Edit > Preferences in Windows) allows you to select a different folder for preset files.

To apply a preset to a picture, select the picture, and then click the Load Preset button (⬗) at the top of the Picture Effects pane. Once you've applied a preset to a picture, you can change settings, make additional adjustments, and apply other filters.

Exporting modified pictures

All of the changes you make to a picture using the Picture Effects pane are saved as part of the project file and are applied to the original (unmodified) picture file for onscreen display and printing. If you want, you can use the Save Picture command (File menu) to create new graphic files that include the adjustments and filters you've applied to pictures within QuarkXPress, and you have the option to link exported pictures to the layout (and disregard the original picture file).

You can also save imported bitmap pictures (for example, .tif and .jpg pictures) that you've modified within QuarkXPress by scaling, cropping, and so on. (You can't save Photoshop files or vector graphics.)

To export the selected picture or all pictures in a layout:

1. Choose File > Save Picture. To save only the selected picture, choose Selected Picture from the submenu; to save all modified pictures in the layout, choose All Pictures in Layout. (If you choose All Pictures in Layout, only pictures in compatible formats and color modes are exported and you'll be warned if the layout contains unsupported graphics.)

2. Modify the settings in the Picture Export Options dialog box (**Figure 7.12**) to suit your needs. Options include the ability to specify resolution, change or retain the color mode and file format, and overwrite the original picture file. If you want the layout to use the exported picture file instead of the original graphic file, check Link Layout to New Picture.

3. Click OK to export the selected picture or all modified pictures in the layout (depending on your choice in Step 1).

FIGURE 7.12 Picture Export Options dialog box.

TIP: **SAVING MULTIPLE PICTURES**

To save some but not all pictures, choose Utilities > Usage, display the Vista pane, select the pictures you want to export, and then click Render.

Managing imported pictures

It's important to understand that when you import a picture into a layout, the picture file is not saved as part of the QuarkXPress project file. Instead, QuarkXPress saves the location of the picture file with the project file and uses the original file for onscreen display and printing. If a picture is modified, moved, deleted, or renamed after you've imported it into a layout, you'll receive a warning when you print the layout or export it as a PDF file.

It's a good idea to check the status of the pictures in a layout from time to time—especially before printing—to make sure that the links to all imported picture files are still intact and that the most recent versions of all picture files are being used.

The Pictures pane (**Figure 7.13**) in the Usage dialog box (Utilities > Usage) displays a list of all imported pictures and lets you correct a couple of common problems. The scroll list shows every instance of each imported picture, as well as the page number, file type, and status of the link between the layout and the picture. For each picture, the Status menu displays one of three possible conditions:

- **OK** means exactly what it implies. The picture file is still in its original location, and the picture hasn't been modified since it was imported. If all pictures are OK, you won't receive any warnings about missing or modified pictures when you print or export the layout.

- **Modified** means that the picture has been modified since it was imported. To update a modified picture, select the file in the list, and then click the Update button.

- **Missing** means that the original picture file is no longer in the location it was in when the file was imported. (The file may have been moved, renamed, or deleted.) To correct this problem, select the file in the list, and then click the Update button. Locate and select the original picture file, and then click Open.

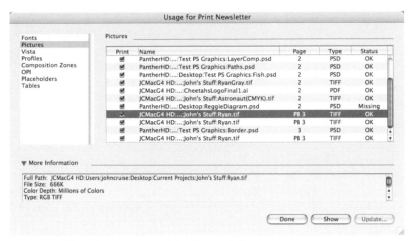

FIGURE 7.13 The Pictures pane of the Usage dialog box.

It's possible to print and export a layout even if it contains missing or modified pictures; however, in these cases QuarkXPress will use low-resolution and outdated versions of modified pictures and low-res versions of missing pictures.

CHAPTER 8

Color

IF YOUR PRINT BUDGET ALLOWS, adding color to a publication can make the difference between ordinary and extraordinary. QuarkXPress includes several features that enable you to design multicolor publications. In this chapter, you'll learn how to create several kinds of colors—including process, spot, and multiple-ink colors—and how to apply colors to text, items, and pictures. You'll also discover how to apply two-color blends to box backgrounds, how to manage the colors in a layout, and how to set up basic color management to ensure that onscreen color display matches print output as closely as possible.

Creating new colors

Every new print layout includes six default colors: cyan, magenta, yellow, and black—the four inks used in process-color printing—plus white and registration, which is a special-purpose color used for printing elements such as crop marks and registration marks. These colors are listed in the Colors palette (Window > Colors; Figure 8.1).

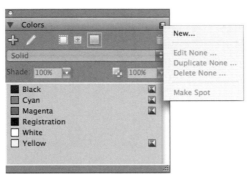

FIGURE 8.1 The Colors palette displays a list of all available colors in a layout. This example shows the six default colors.

You can add as many additional colors as you want to a layout, and all colors you add to a layout are available to all layouts in the project. To add a color:

1. Choose New from the Colors palette menu, click the New color button 🔃 at the top left of the palette, or choose Edit > Color. If you choose Edit > Color, click New in the Edit Color dialog box to display the New Color dialog box (Figure 8.2).

2. In the Edit Color dialog box, it's usually best to select a (Color) Model before you specify a name. The controls on the right half of the dialog box change depending on the color model you choose. If you choose a commercial color model—for example, one of the PANTONE or Toyo models—and then select a color, the color name/number is automatically placed in the Name field. You can always enter whatever name you want in the Name field. Figures 8.2 and 8.3 show examples of CMYK and spot colors. For more information about color models, see the sidebar "About Color Models."

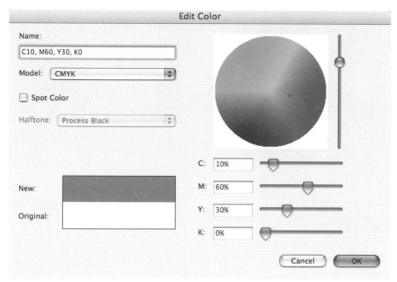

FIGURE 8.2 This example shows how to create a CMYK color. The custom name is intended to show the percentage of the color's cyan, magenta, yellow, and black components.

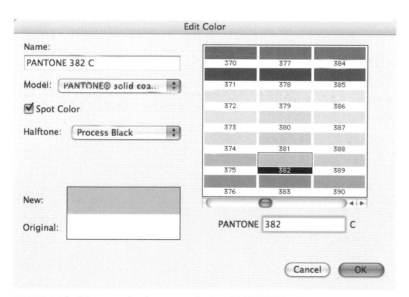

FIGURE 8.3 In this example, the new color is a PANTONE® solid coated spot color (PANTONE 382 C). When selecting a PANTONE color, you can click a color swatch in the list or enter a number in the PANTONE field.

3. Check Spot Color if you want the color to print on a single color separation plate. If Spot Color is not checked, the color will be separated into process colors if you print color separations. In general, when you choose a color model, you should accept the Spot Color setting. For example, if you choose CMYK, Spot Color is not checked. If you check Spot Color for a CMYK color, it will print as a spot color on its own color separation plate.

4. Optional: If you check Spot Color, the selection you make from the Halftone menu determines the screen angle that's used to print shades of the spot color.

After you add a color to a layout, it's displayed in the Colors palette and you're ready to apply it to text and items.

About color models

You may be surprised and somewhat overwhelmed the first time you click the Model menu in the Edit Color dialog box (Figure 8.3) and discover that there are 25 choices. Don't worry. Many are commercially available printing inks, and others are Web-specific colors. Here's a brief description of the choices:

- **Commercial inks:** DIC, FOCOLTONE, PANTONE, TOYO, and TRUMATCH are all manufacturers of printing inks. Some of the color models that bear these names are made up of spot colors—for example, PANTONE® solid coated and TOYO—while other commercial color models include only CMYK/process colors. PANTONE® process uncoated, FOCOLTONE, and TRUMATCH are examples. If you choose a spot color model, the Spot Color check box is selected; if you choose a CMYK color model, the Spot Color check box is not selected.

- **CMYK:** If you choose the CMYK color model, you can specify the percentage of cyan, magenta, yellow, and black. If possible, you should use a process color swatchbook when you create a CMYK color. These swatchbooks include printed examples and CMYK percentages for each color so that you know exactly what the color looks like when printed.

- **Multi-ink colors:** A multi-ink color is a combination of two or more spot or process colors. Multi-ink colors are often used in two-color publications (black plus a spot color) and are created by combining the spot color (or a percentage of the spot color) with black (or a percentage of black). Using multi-ink colors is a good way to increase the number of hues in a publication without adding more colors and jacking up the printing cost. (See the sidebar below for more about multi-ink colors.)

RGB colors: The RGB (red, green, blue) color model is used to display color on computer monitors and other video displays (televisions, mobile phones, and such) and is also the color model used for Web pages and Web graphics. If you add RGB colors to a print layout, CMYK equivalents of the RGB values are used when you print the document to a color printer or print color separations.

Web colors: Web Safe Colors and Web Named Colors are for use in Web layouts.

HSB and LAB colors. Neither of these color models is appropriate for print layouts, so you probably won't be using them. The HSB (hue, saturation, brightness) color model defines a color based on its color (hue), the intensity of the color (saturation), and the value of the color (brightness). The LAB color model is a standardized model for representing colors that can be used to convert colors between the RGB and CMYK color models.

Using multi-ink colors is a good way to expand the number of hues in a two-color layout without adding colors and incurring additional expense at the printer. Because this book is a two-color publication (black plus a spot color), it provides an opportunity to demonstrate multi-ink colors in action.

The topmost box on the right is filled with a PANTONE spot color, specifically a 100% shade of PANTONE 382 C from the PANTONE® process coated swatchbook. The box on the bottom is 100% black. The four boxes in between are filled with four separate multi-ink colors that combine a 100% shade of PANTONE 382 C with increasing shades of black (15%, 30%, 50%, and 75%).

Applying color

You can apply color to just about anything in a layout, including text, box backgrounds, frames, lines, drop shadows, paragraph rules, and imported black-and-white and grayscale pictures and their backgrounds. Imported color pictures are the only elements to which you can't apply color.

QuarkXPress provides three options for applying colors to items: the Modify dialog box (Item > Modify), the Colors palette, and the Measurements palette. The examples in this section show how to apply colors using the Colors palette, but nearly all of the same controls are available in the Modify dialog box and the Measurements palette, so you can use the one you prefer.

To apply color to text:

1. Highlight the text to which you want to apply color.

2. Choose Window > Colors to display the Colors palette (**Figure 8.4**) if it's not already open.

3. Click the Text Color button , and then click a color in the list.

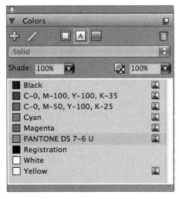

FIGURE 8.4 In this example, a process color named PANTONE DS 7-6 U (from the PANTONE® process uncoated color model) is applied to the text. The CMYK icons ◨ to the right of color names in the Colors palette indicate that these colors are process colors.

The controls for applying color to text are also available in the Classic and Character Attributes tabs of the Measurements palette and the Style menu (Style > Color). The Modify dialog box does not include controls for applying color to text.

Applying color to other elements is much the same as applying color to text:

- **Box background:** Select the box (text, picture, or no content) to which you want to apply a background color. Click the Background Color button ◼ in the Colors palette, and then click a color in the list. The Box pane in the Modify dialog box and the Classic tab of the Measurements palette also include controls for applying color to box backgrounds.

- **Frame:** Select a box. Click the Frame Color button ▣ in the Colors palette, and then click a color in the list. The Frame pane in the Modify dialog box and the Frame tab of the Measurements palette also include controls for applying color to frames. If the frame style is dashed or striped, you can also specify a color for the gap areas. Gap Color controls are available in the Classic tab of the Measurements palette and the Frame pane of the Modify dialog box, though not in the Colors palette.

- **Line:** Select a line. Click the Line Color button ▨ in the Colors palette, and then click a color in the list. The Line pane in the Modify dialog box and the Classic tab of the Measurements palette also include controls for applying color to lines. If the line is dashed or striped, you can also specify a color for the gap areas in the Line pane of the Modify dialog box, though not in the Colors palette.

- **Picture:** Select a picture box that contains a black-and-white or grayscale picture. The graphic file must be a bitmap format (for example, .tif or .jpg). Click the Picture Color button ▣ in the Colors palette (be careful not to click the Picture Background Color button ▣ instead), and then click a color in the list. If you click the Picture Background color button, you can apply a color to the selected picture's background. The Picture pane in the Modify dialog box also includes controls for applying color to pictures and picture backgrounds, though not in the Measurements palette.

Dragging and dropping colors

In addition to the aforementioned options for applying color to items, you can also drag a color from the Colors palette and drop it onto any element to which color can be applied. (You can't use the drag-and-drop method to apply color to a picture or a picture background.) As you drag a color, the color is instantly used to display each element the swatch touches—frame, box background, line, and so on. Release the mouse to apply the color to the currently colorized element.

Changing shade and opacity

QuarkXPress offers two options for lightening any color that you've applied to an item: You can assign a shade value, an opacity value, or any combination of both. It's important to understand that when you assign a shade value (other than 100%) to an item, the item becomes lighter but remains opaque (that is, it obstructs the visibility of all items that are below it in the stacking order). When you assign an opacity value (other than 100%) to an item, the item becomes lighter and translucent, revealing items that are below it in the stacking order.

Shade and Opacity controls are available in all places where color controls are available. You can apply shade and opacity values between 100% and 0%.

An item becomes increasingly lighter as you lower its shade value. A shade value of 0% makes an item invisible. As a general rule, you shouldn't apply a shade value of less than 5% to an item because it might not be visible when printed. It's best to check with your print service provider if you intend to print a publication that uses very light shades.

An item becomes increasingly lighter and transparent as you lower its opacity value. An opacity value of 0% makes an item invisible. The same caveat that applies to shade values applies to opacity values. Very low values may result in items that don't print.

Applying two-color blends to box backgrounds

A blend is a smooth transition between two colors. QuarkXPress lets you apply two-color blends to box backgrounds (though not to any other elements). Adding blended boxes to a layout can provide contrast, movement, and visual appeal. To apply a two-color blend to a box background.

1. Select a box (text, picture, or no content) with the Item tool.

2. Click the Background Color button ▇ in the Colors palette.

3. Choose an option other than Solid from the menu of blend styles (just below the row of buttons along the top of the palette). The choices are Linear Blend, Mid-Linear Blend, Rectangular Blend, Diamond Blend, Circular Blend, and Full Circular Blend. Figure 8.5 includes an example of each blend style.

4. To specify the first color in the blend, click the #1 button, and then click a color in the list.

5. To specify the second color in the blend, click the #2 button, and then click a color in the list.

6. Optional: To change the angle of the blend, enter a value between 360° and -360° in the Angle field.

7. Optional: You can assign a Shade value or an Opacity for each color in the blend.

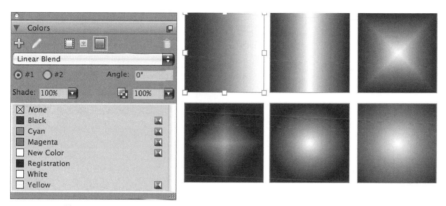

FIGURE 8.5 If you choose a blend style from the menu of choices, three additional controls are added to the Colors palette: #1 (Color) button, #2 (Color) button, and Angle field. In this example, Linear Blend is applied to the selected box at the top left. The other five blend styles are applied to the other boxes: (top row) Mid-Linear Blend, Rectangular Blend; (bottom row) Diamond Blend, Circular Blend, and Full Circular Blend.

Managing the colors in a layout

In addition to allowing you to apply colors to items, the Colors palette also offers a few options for managing the colors in a layout, including the four commands in the palette menu:

- **New:** Opens the New Color dialog box.

- **Edit [Color Name]:** Opens the Edit Color dialog box, which allows you to change the settings of the selected color. You can also click the Edit button at the top left of the Colors palette to open the Edit Color dialog box.

- **Delete:** Deletes the color that's currently selected in the palette. If you delete a color that's used in the layout, you are given the option of replacing the deleted color with an existing color.

- **Duplicate:** Creates a copy of the color that's currently selected in the palette that you can then use as the starting point for a variation of the selected color.

- **Make Process/Make Spot:** If a spot color is selected in the palette, choose Make Process to convert it to a process (CMYK) color; if a process color is selected, choose Make Spot to convert it to a spot color.

Additional options for managing colors are available in the Colors for [Name of Layout] dialog box (**Edit > Colors; Figure 8.6**). In addition to the New, Edit, Duplicate, and Delete buttons, the other options are:

- **Append:** Allows you to import the colors from another project. Click Append to open the Append Colors dialog box, which allows you to choose a project file. After you choose a project file, click Open to display the Append Colors dialog box, which allows you to select the colors you want to import.

- **Edit Trap:** Trapping is a printing technique in which abutting color items are printed with a slight overlap to ensure that gaps don't occur (and the paper isn't visible) between the items if misregistration occurs on the press. Click Edit Trap to open the Trap Specifications for [Name of Color] dialog box, which allows you to specify trapping values for the selected color relative to the other colors in the layout. Unless you're a color expert, it's a good idea to let your print service provider handle trapping-related tasks.

FIGURE 8.6 The Colors for [Name of Color] dialog box displays a list of the colors in a layout and provides several controls for managing the colors.

CHANGING DEFAULT COLORS

If you want to add any colors to the list of six default colors (black, cyan, magenta, registration, white, and yellow), close all projects and then add the colors. Any colors you create when no projects are open are added to the list of default colors and are available in all new projects. If you have a corporate spot color or an in-house palette of preferred colors, you might want to add them to the default list.

In much the same way that you can search for and replace text (Edit > Find/Change), you can also search for and replace colors. Choose Edit > Item Find/Change to display the Item Find/Change dialog box (**Figure 8.7**). All of the panes in this dialog box (with the exception of the Box pane) include controls for finding and changing color, shade, and opacity. The Box Color pane also includes controls for finding and changing backgrounds with two-color blends. You can adjust the settings in as many panes as you want (for example, you can find and change box color and frame color in a single operation). The Summary pane displays all of the search and replace criteria.

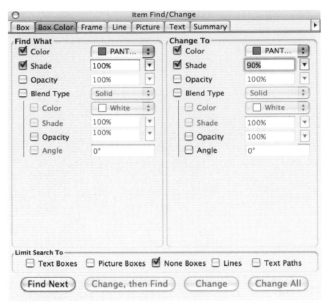

FIGURE 8.7 The Item Find/Change dialog box lets you search for and replace many item attributes, including colors.

Setting up basic color management

The color management process attempts to overcome the differences in the way various vendors and equipment—such as digital cameras, scanners, monitors, and printers—reproduce colors. If you've ever bought something from a Web site, you know that the color you see onscreen and the actual color of the item can vary significantly. That's because the colors onscreen are displayed with a mixture of red, green, and blue light while the original image, probably shot for a print catalog, reproduces the colors with cyan, magenta, yellow, and black dots. Color management systems work by translating color definitions among devices and simulating the best color possible for each output device.

Big, thick books have been written about color management, and the science and physiology behind color and the human eye are the stuff of college courses. Most designers, however, avoid color management and rely on their experience with various types of images, paper, printers, and inks. But you don't have to be a color expert to set up basic color management with QuarkXPress 8. The default color management environment simulates color output in various output scenarios with minimal user input. In addition, QuarkXPress 8 offers experts granular controls for designing a color management system tailored specifically to an individual workflow.

TIP: **EXPERT SOURCE SETUPS AND OUTPUT SETUPS**

In a high-end publishing environment in which color is crucial, a color expert or a printer may provide packages of color management settings called source setups and output setups. You can append or import these setups and use them while importing pictures, viewing color onscreen, and printing both proofs and final color separations. For more information about using source setups and output setups in a color-managed workflow, see the QXP User Guide.pdf (QuarkXPress program folder > Documents > English).

Calibrating your devices

The number one thing you can do to display and output better color is to calibrate your monitors and printers. While this has nothing to do with QuarkXPress specifically, it has everything to do with the results onscreen and on press. In Windows, you'll need to use calibration software provided with the monitor or laptop. If you have a Mac, you can use the Color tab in the Displays System Preference (System Preferences > Displays > Color). For printers, check the documentation for calibration information. And remember, devices don't stay calibrated forever. If you move a computer to a different office with more light or you install new toner cartridges in a printer, you may need to calibrate again.

Choosing your monitor profile

A monitor profile defines how your computer's screen displays colors. QuarkXPress consults this profile, selected in Preferences > Application > Display > Monitor Profile (**Figure 8.8**), to display the best possible colors. By default, the monitor profile is set to Automatic, which is the profile for the monitor that your system recognizes. (For example, Automatic for an iMac means that the iMac monitor profile is in effect.) You might select a different profile in a high-end color management workflow, if you have two monitors and primarily view color on the second monitor, or you want to match the color between a desktop computer and a laptop.

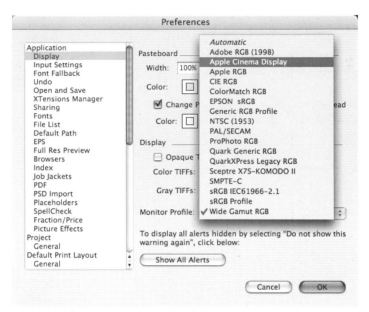

FIGURE 8.8 You can choose a different monitor profile in the Display tab of the Preferences dialog box to simulate other color-viewing environments.

Working with profiles

Simply calibrating your monitor and working in the default QuarkXPress environment offers decent color throughout a workflow. If you're working in an expert color management environment, however, you'll be using profiles. Color management profiles are little files that define how colors are produced: whether they're RGB or CMYK, which vendor created them, and much more. The easiest way to see profiles at work is with pictures.

1. In the Preferences dialog box, click the Color Manager tab under Print Layout.

2. Under Source Options, check Enable Access to Picture Profiles, then click OK.

3. Choose File > Import. Select a picture file and notice the Color Management tab at the bottom of the dialog box (**Figure 8.9**). This lets you define the source of the picture (Profile) and how the color will best display (Rendering Intent). Click Open to import the picture.

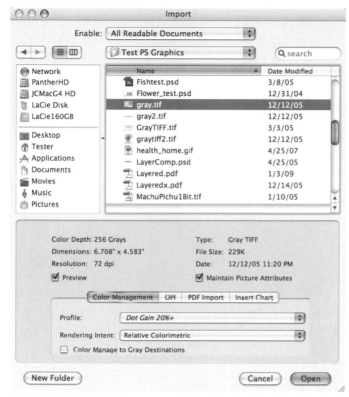

FIGURE 8.9 The Color Management tab of the Import dialog box lets you identify the source of a picture and how it will best display.

4. Choose Window > Profile Information. You can use the Profile Information palette to change the profile and rendering intent of the selected picture.

5. To see all the profiles used in a layout, choose Utilities > Usage, then click Profiles. You can manage the profiles used in a layout from here, including globally replacing profiles in all pictures.

Proofing color onscreen

QuarkXPress 8 lets you quickly proof colors in various output scenarios—for example, if you're printing a grayscale version of an ad or converting a spot (such as a PANTONE) color to its process (CMYK) equivalent. Choose View > Proof Output to see the options (Figure 8.10). The entire layout, including the Colors palette, will display according to the Proof Output option selected.

FIGURE 8.10 Use View > Proof Output to view a simulation of output to different devices. Here, an RGB.tif file displays as grayscale to see how it will look in the newspaper.

CHAPTER 9

Pages

EACH TIME YOU CREATE A NEW QUARKXPRESS PRINT LAYOUT, page 1 of the layout is displayed in a window that includes the pasteboard (the area that surrounds the page), rulers along the top and left edges, and several controls along the bottom edge. (For more about the program's user interface, see Chapter 2.) At this point, you're ready to begin working on your publication. However, if you intend to create a multipage publication, you'll probably want to do a little preparatory work before you begin creating text boxes and picture boxes, formatting text, and so on. In particular, it's a good idea to set up layout-wide guidelines and add the required number of pages before you begin working on the individual pages. Even if you're designing a single-page publication, you might want to establish some guidelines on the page to help you place the items it will contain.

In this chapter you'll learn how to add gridlines and guidelines to your pages, how to set up master pages that function as templates for the layout pages, how to specify page numbering, how to divide a layout into independently numbered sections, and how to add, delete, and move pages within a layout. You'll also learn how to use layers to organize the items on your pages.

Each time you create a new print layout—either when you open a new project or when you add a layout to an existing project—you specify margin and column settings in the New Project and New Layout dialog boxes. The settings you make are used for the margin and column guidelines displayed on page 1 (they're blue by default). These settings are also used for pages you add to the layout. The purpose of these nonprinting guidelines is to help you arrange and align items on a page and, in the case of margin guides, to remind you of the boundary of the editorial area on a page.

If you want, you can change the original margin and column settings, and you also have the option to use different margin and column settings for different pages in the layout. For example, if you're creating a newsletter, you might want to use a two-column layout for some pages and a three-column layout for others. Before we explain how to modify margin and column settings, you need to understand a very important QuarkXPress feature: master pages. (You'll learn much more about master pages later in this chapter.)

Understanding master pages

Each time you create a new layout, page 1 is displayed in the project window. What is not immediately apparent is that every layout also contains another, nonprinting page—called a master page—that has some unique and important properties that you need to know about if you're going to be creating multipage publications. If you're creating a one-page publication (a poster or a business card, for example), you don't need to be concerned with a layout's master page because there's no need to use it—even though it's part of the layout.

A master page serves as the background for the pages in a layout. Any changes you make to a master page are applied to all pages in the layout that are based on that master page. Master pages typically include such elements as page numbers, headers, and footers—that is, items that are common to all pages.

To make changes to a layout's master page, you must first display it. To display a layout's master page, choose Window > Page Layout to open the Page Layout palette (**Figure 9.1**), and then double-click on the A-Master A icon at the top of the palette (just below the row of icons). For facing-page layouts, the master page icon has dog-ears at the top corners to indicate that the master page is actually a two-page spread with a left-page component (sometimes called a verso page) and a right-page (recto page) component.

Although each new layout initially includes only one master page, you can create additional master pages if you want to use different page designs within a single publication. You'll learn more about master pages, including how to add new ones to a layout, later in this chapter.

FIGURE 9.1 The Page Layout palette. Layout page icons are displayed in the lower portion of the palette; master page icons are displayed in the area above the layout pages. The buttons at the top of the palette let you add, duplicate, and delete master pages and divide a layout into independently numbered sections.

Distinguishing a master page spread from a layout page spread can be a little tricky, especially for pages that don't yet contain any items. There are some visual cues in the project window that indicate whether you're viewing a master page or a layout page (**Figure 9.2**):

- When a master page is displayed in the project window, the name of the page appears in the lower-left corner of the project window. For example, L-A-Master A is displayed when the left page of the master page named A-Master A is showing. When a layout page is displayed, its page number is appears in the lower-left corner.

- When a master page is displayed in the project window, either a linked chain icon (⟳) or an unlinked chain icon (⟳) is displayed in the upper-left corner of each component (verso page and recto page). The linked chain icon indicates that the page includes an automatic text box; the unlinked chain icon indicates that the page doesn't include an automatic text box. (For more about using automatic text boxes to flow text, see Chapter 4.)

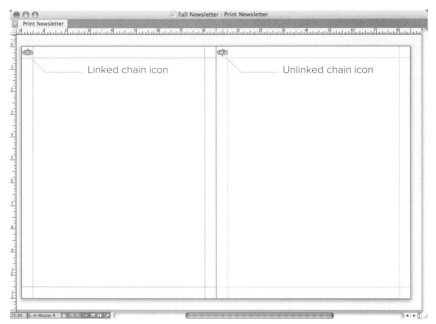

FIGURE 9.2 The linked chain icons in the upper-left corners of the verso and recto master page components indicate that you're viewing a master page spread and not a layout page spread.

One of the most common mistakes of QuarkXPress novices is thinking they're modifying a layout page when they're actually working on a master page and vice versa. If you realize you've done this, you can undo your recent actions, or you can simply cut the items from the incorrect page and paste them onto the correct page (choose Edit > Paste in Place to maintain the location of the copied items).

Changing margins and columns

The preceding explanation of master pages is necessary because if you want to change a layout's columns, margins, and other basic attributes, you must do so by making the changes to the layout's master page.

To change a layout's margins and columns:

1. Make sure that the layout's master page is displayed in the project window. If the layout has more than one master page, check that the one you want to modify is displayed.

2. Choose Page > Master Guides & Grid.

3. In the Master Guides & Grid dialog box (**Figure 9.3**), change the settings in the Margin Guides or Column Guides section. In the Margin Guides section, the icons to the right of the Top/Bottom and Inside/Outside fields let you adjust each pair of fields separately or as one. When the chain is not broken 🔗, changing the value in one field also changes the value in the other; when the chain is broken 🔗, you can enter different values in each field.

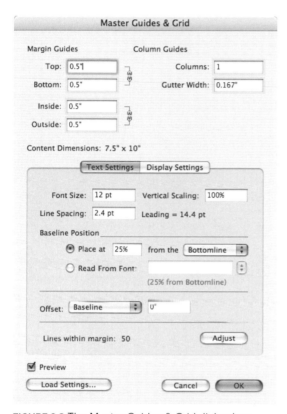

FIGURE 9.3 The Master Guides & Grid dialog box.

TIP: *MULTICOLUMN TEXT BOXES*

When you create a new text box, it includes a single column. If you want to divide a text box into multiple, equal-width columns, open the Modify dialog box, and then change the number in the Text pane's Columns field.

If you change margin guide or column guide settings for a master page that includes an automatic text box and the edges of the text box coincide with the margins, your changes are also applied to the automatic text box. For example, changing the number of columns on a master page also changes the number of columns in the automatic text box.

Using master page grids

In QuarkXPress gridlines are nonprinting, horizontal lines that you can use to help position and align text baselines, item edges, and other elements as you lay out pages. In early versions of QuarkXPress, each document had a single, document-wide "baseline grid"; however, recent versions of QuarkXPress have greatly expanded on the baseline grid feature—to the point that trying to cover all available controls is beyond the scope of this book. Fortunately, you can take advantage of page grids without knowing or using all of the choices.

In QuarkXPress 8, each master page includes a page grid. If a layout has multiple master pages, you can use the same page grid for all master pages, or you can create multiple page grids and assign them to whatever master pages you want. To view a layout's page grid, choose View > Page Grid. (Choose the same command again to hide the grid.)

Like master guides and column guides, you must display a layout's master page if you want to change the page grid for all pages in the layout. To change a layout's page grid:

1. Make sure that the layout's master page is displayed in the project window. If the layout has more than one master page, make sure the one you want to modify is displayed.

2. Choose Page > Master Guides & Grid.

3. Select the Preview box in the Master Guides & Grid dialog box to view changes as you make them.

4. Adjust the settings in the Text Settings pane (**Figure 9.4**). Typically, the Font Size value is equal to the font size of the publication's body text, and the Line Spacing value is the amount of vertical space that's added to the Font Size for each line of type (Font Size plus Line Spacing equals Leading).

5. Optional: If you want to specify the position of text baselines based on the built-in specifications of a particular font (usually the body copy font), select Read From Font, and then select a font from the accompanying menu. (A text baseline is a horizontal line along which the bottom edge of letters align.)

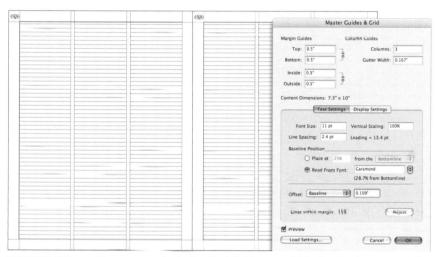

FIGURE 9.4 The settings you make in the Text Settings and Display Settings panes determine the placement and appearance of gridlines.

TIP: *LOADING GRID SETTINGS*

The Load Settings button in the Master Guides & Grid dialog box lets you use an existing master page grid, paragraph style sheet, or grid style (grid styles are covered in the next section) as the basis for a master page grid. Click Load Settings in the Master Guides & Grid dialog box to display a list of the layout's master page grids, grid styles, and paragraph style sheets. Choose the one you want to use, and then click OK.

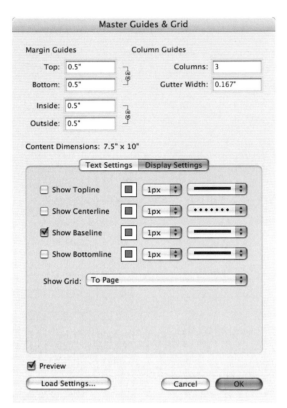

FIGURE 9.5 The settings you make in the Text Settings and Display Settings panes determine the placement and appearance of gridlines.

6. Optional: Click Display Settings to activate a different set of controls (**Figure 9.5**) that enables you to show or hide four text-related gridlines: toplines, centerlines, baselines, and bottomlines. The options in the Show Grid menu let you extend the gridlines to the page edges or beyond to the pasteboard. While it's nice to be able to display so many different kinds of gridlines, the more you display, the denser and more distracting they become.

TIP: *TEXT BOX GRIDS*

In addition to page-based grids, you can also create grids for text boxes. To create a text box grid, Control+click (Mac) or right-click (Windows) on a text box, and then use the controls in the Grid Settings dialog box—which are almost identical to the controls in the Text Settings and Display Settings panes in the Master Guides & Grid dialog box—to specify the grid settings.

Grid styles

Much like paragraph style sheets, character style sheets, and item styles, a grid style is a set of grid attributes that you can assign to master pages and text boxes. Using grid styles saves time and ensures consistency.

To create a grid style:

1. Choose Edit > Grid Styles.

2. Click New in the Edit Grid Styles for [Layout Name] dialog box.

3. In the Edit Grid Style dialog box, assign a name to the grid style, and then use the controls in the Text Settings and Display Settings panes to configure the style.

4. Optional: To base the grid style on an existing master page grid, a paragraph style sheet, or another grid style, click Load Settings in the Edit Grid Style dialog box, choose a option from the list, and then click OK.

TIP: *NORMAL GRID STYLE/NORMAL PARAGRAPH STYLE SHEET*

Because all layouts include the Normal paragraph style sheet and this style sheet is automatically applied to new text boxes, some QuarkXPress users like to use the Normal paragraph style for a layout's body text. When you create a new grid style, checking Link to Paragraph Style Normal uses the text settings of the Normal paragraph style as the basis for the grid style.

To apply a grid style to a selected text box:

1. Choose Window > Grid Styles to display the Grid Styles palette.

2. Click a grid style in the list of styles.

Using ruler guides

Ruler guides are nonprinting guidelines that you create manually on an as-needed basis to help you position and align items on pages. To add a horizontal guide to a page:

1. Make sure rulers are displayed along the top and left sides of the project window. If not, choose View > Rulers to display them.

2. Click the horizontal ruler at the top of the window and drag the pointer downward. As you drag, the ‡ pointer is displayed. Release the pointer over a page to draw a horizontal guide that spans only that page; release the pointer over the pasteboard to draw a horizontal guideline that spans both pages of a spread and the pasteboard. If you want to place the guideline at a specific distance from the top edge of the page, keep your eye on the Y: field in the Measurements palette as you drag and release the mouse button when the correct value is displayed.

Creating a vertical guide is the same as creating a horizontal guide except you click the vertical ruler at the left side of the project window. As you drag, the ↔ pointer is displayed. Keep your eye on the X: field in the Measurements palette if you want to place the guideline a specific distance from the left edge of the page.

To remove a rule guide, click it with the Item tool and drag it back to its ruler of origin.

Modifying ruler guides

Ruler guides are somewhat like items—text boxes, picture boxes, and so on—in that you can modify several attributes. To modify a ruler guide, click it with the Item tool; double-click if an item is in front of the guide. The controls in the Guide Attributes dialog box (**Figure 9.6**) let you change the location and direction of the guide, its length (Page width or Spread width plus pasteboard), and its color. The View Scale Value determines the magnification at which the guide is visible. (The guide is visible at view percentages equal to and above the View Scale value.) If you check Locked, you won't be able to move or delete the guide until you unlock it.

FIGURE 9.6 The Guide Attributes dialog box lets you configure several properties of ruler guides.

If you'd like even more ways to control guides than the ones available in the Guide Attributes dialog box, you'll find several additional options in the Guides palette

(Window > Guides; **Figure 9.7**). When a layout page is displayed in the project window, the Guides palette displays a page-by-page list of all ruler guides in the layout. When a master page is displayed in the project window, the Guides palette displays a list of all master page ruler guides.

The controls along the top of the Guides palette let you add, mirror, and control the display of guides. (When you mirror a guide, it is moved to the opposite side of the page it's on. After mirroring, the repositioned guide is the same distance from the center of the page as the original guide.) Several more commands for working with guides are available in the palette menu. For example, you can copy and paste guides, create grids, and import and export guides.

If you want to modify a particular guide, select it in the list. When a guide is selected, you can modify the settings in the Location, Color, (View) Scale, and (Show/Hide) columns.

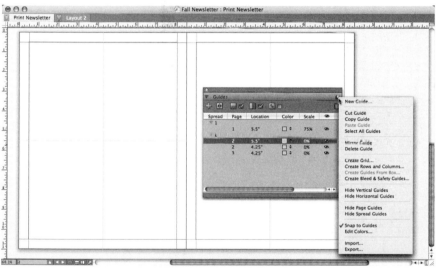

FIGURE 9.7 The Guides palette displays a list of all ruler guides in a layout and lets you select and modify individual guides.

Managing guides and grids

QuarkXPress provides several features that help you manage guidelines and page grids and use them efficiently as you lay out pages.

Guides and grid preferences

You can change the default settings for a layout's margin guides, ruler guides, and page grids by modifying the settings in the Guides & Grid pane of the Preferences dialog box (QuarkXPress > Preferences in Mac systems; Edit > Preferences in Windows; Figure 9.8). Among other things, you can specify the color of margin and ruler guides and choose between displaying guides and grids in front of or behind items. Each layout in a project uses its own preference settings.

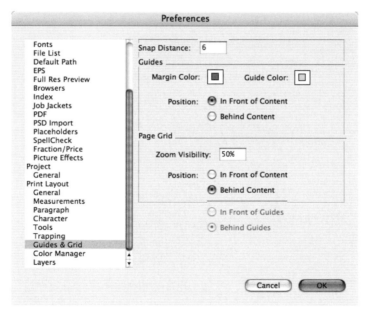

FIGURE 9.8 The controls in the Guides & Grid pane of the Preferences dialog box let you establish default settings for margin and ruler guides and page grids.

Showing/hiding, snapping to guides and grids

The View menu includes three commands for controlling the display of guides and grids:

- **Guides:** Alternately shows and hides margin guides and ruler guides.

- **Page Grids:** Alternately shows and hides page grids.

- **Text Box Grids:** Alternately shows and hides grids applied to text boxes.

Two additional commands let you control whether item edges snap to guidelines and gridlines when you create, resize, and move items:

- **Snap to Guides:** When this command is checked, the edges of items will snap to (align with) margin and ruler guides when an item edge gets within 6 pixels of a guide as you drag. Select the command when it's checked to turn off snapping to guides.

- **Snap to Page Grids:** When this command is checked, the edges of items will snap to gridlines when an item edge gets within six pixels of a gridline as you drag. Select the command when it's checked to turn off snapping to page grids.

You can change the default snap distance of 6 pixels by changing the value in the Snap Distance field in the Guides & Grid pane of the Preferences dialog box.

Working with master pages

As was mentioned earlier in this chapter, master pages are extremely useful for multipage publications. By placing items on master pages, you save yourself the time and effort of creating every page from scratch and you ensure consistency across all pages in the publication.

The main difference between master pages and the actual (nonmaster) pages in a layout is that a master page contains only items that appear on all layout pages based on that master—headers, footers, page numbers, and such. Laying out a master page is the same as laying out a nonmaster page. You use the item-creation tools to place items on the page, and then you modify these items as needed. (For more information about creating and modifying items, see Chapter 3.)

Creating new master pages

For some publications, a single master page may be all that's required. For example, a simple four-page newsletter may have only a single facing-page master with a three-column layout. Other publications may require additional master pages. If you want to add a little variety to a three-column newsletter, you can create an additional master page with a two-column layout. You can then use either the three-column master page or the two-column master page as the background for the pages of the newsletter.

To create a new master page:

1. Choose Window > Page Layout to display the Page Layout palette if it's not already open.

2. Choose New Single Page Master or New Facing Page Master from the Page Layout palette's menu (**Figure 9.9**). (Generally, you'll choose New Facing Page Master for publications with facing pages.)

The new master page is added to the list of master pages at the top of the Page Layout palette and assigned a name. To rename the master page, click its name in the list, and then enter a new name in the field. Master page names must begin with a single number or letter followed by a hyphen (for example, A- or 1-).

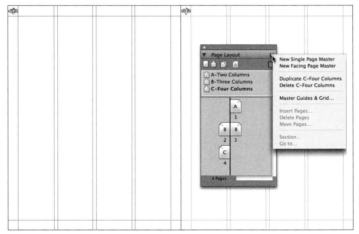

FIGURE 9.9 Page Layout palette. In this example, the palette shows that the layout has three facing-page master pages, each with a different number of columns. The master page named C-Four Columns is visible behind the palette. The four pages in the lower portion of the palette are layout pages, and the letter on each page indicates the master page that's applied. Master page A-Two Column is applied to page 1, B-Three Column is applied to pages 2 and 3, and C-Four Column is applied to page 4.

After you create a new master page, double-click the page icon to the left of its name in the Page Layout palette to display it in the project window. Choose View > 50% or

View > 75% and scroll if necessary so that you can see both pages of a facing-page master. At this point you're ready to begin adding items to the master page. If you want to change the margins, columns, or page grid, choose Page > Master Guides & Grid, and then adjust the settings in the Master Guides & Grid dialog box.

TIP: **MASTER ITEMS VS. NONMASTER ITEMS**

Any item you place on a master page is also placed on all layout pages based on that master page. Master items on layout pages behave the same as other (nonmaster) items you've added to the page. Selecting and modifying master items on layout pages is the same as selecting and modifying nonmaster items; however, if you modify a master item on a layout page, the item is no longer a master item. If you then modify the original item on the master page, the changes are not applied to the item you modified on the layout page. If you want to prevent a master item from being moved or modified (on both the master page and layout pages based on that master page), select it on the master page, and then choose Item > Lock.

After you've finished working on a master page, you can apply it to new or existing pages in the layout. The next section explains how to add pages to a layout and how to apply master pages to layout pages.

TIP: **CREATING VARIATIONS OF A MASTER PAGE**

Often, the only difference between master pages in a layout with multiple masters is the number of columns. An easy way to ensure consistency across multiple master pages that differ only in the number of columns is to lay out the first master page, copy all of the items, and then paste them onto subsequent master pages. If you choose Edit > Paste in Place, the copied items will maintain their original position on the page. After you've pasted the items onto a new master page, change the column settings in the Master Guides & Grid dialog box.

Adding, deleting, and rearranging pages

After you've set up your guidelines, gridlines, and master pages, you're ready to add pages to your layout and begin designing pages. During the course of production, you may subsequently need to add more pages, delete existing pages, or move pages within the layout.

Adding pages

QuarkXPress offers two methods for adding pages to a layout: the Insert Pages dialog box (**Figure 9.10**) and the Page Layout palette. They're equally straightforward, so use the method that's most convenient for you. To use the dialog box:

1. Choose Page > Insert Pages.

2. In the Insert Pages dialog box, enter the number of pages you want to add in the Insert field, and then choose one of the three options that determine where the pages are inserted. If you choose Before Page or After Page, enter a page number in the accompanying field.

3. Optional: If a text chain is active, you can link it to the automatic text box if you choose a master page (next step) that has one.

4. To base the new pages on a master page, choose one from the Master Page menu. You can also choose Blank Single or Blank Facing Page to insert blank pages.

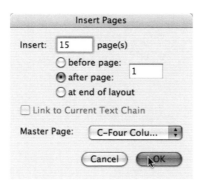

FIGURE 9.10 The Insert Pages dialog lets you add pages to a layout, specify the placement of the pages relative to existing pages, and apply a master page to the new pages.

To insert a single page using the Page Layout palette:

1. Click and drag a master page icon from the top of the palette to the bottom of the palette where layout pages are displayed.

2. Drag the pointer to either side of an existing page, and then release the mouse. Be careful not to release the mouse when a current page is highlighted. If you do, you'll apply the master page to the layout page without creating a new page. If you move the pointer between two existing pages, the page on the left will be pushed to the left if the ⊣ pointer is displayed; the page on the right will be pushed to the right if the ⊢ pointer is displayed.

As you drag a master page icon, you can also move the pointer below any of the page icons and then release the mouse to insert a new page after (rather than to the side of) the existing page.

If you want to add multiple pages using the Page Layout palette, hold down the Option key (Mac) or the Alt key (Windows) as you drag a master page icon to the bottom of the Page Layout palette. When you release the mouse, the Insert Pages dialog box is displayed. You can also choose Insert Pages from the Page Layout palette menu to display the Insert Pages dialog box.

> TIP: **A WORD ABOUT PAGE COUNTS**
>
> *A QuarkXPress layout can contain any number of pages—even or odd; however, real-world print publications always have an even number of pages, and because of binding issues, the total number of pages is almost always a multiple of four. If you're creating a publication that will be commercially printed, ask your printer about the recommended page counts, and make sure that you end up with a viable number of pages in the layout. Or, if your layout is part of a larger publication, check that the page count for the entire publication works.*

*You can add a fold-out page to a facing-page publication by creating a pair of consecutive three-page spreads. **Figure 9.11** shows how it's done and how the pages look in the Page Layout palette. Make sure you work closely with your printer if you create publications that require special handling.*

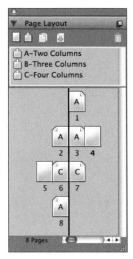

FIGURE 9.11 The blank master pages at the right of page 3 and the left of page 6 produce a fold-out page and two three-page spreads.

Deleting pages

To delete a range of pages, choose Page > Delete, and then specify the page range you want to delete. You can also delete pages using the Page Layout palette. First, select the pages you want to delete, and then click the trash can icon at the top of the palette. To select a range of pages, click the first page, and then Shift+click the last page. To select multiple, nonsequential pages, hold down the Command key (Mac) or the Control key (Windows), and then click the desired pages.

Rearranging pages

Similar to adding and deleting pages, you have two options for rearranging pages within a layout. To move a range of pages:

1. Choose Page > Move.

2. In the Move Pages dialog box (**Figure 9.12**), specify the range of pages you want to move, and then choose one of the three options that determine where the pages are inserted. If you choose Before Page or After Page, enter a page number in the accompanying field.

Move Pages

Move page(s): [   ] thru: [   ]   ○ before page: [ ]
                                         ● after page: [4]
                                         ○ to end of layout

                                         (Cancel) (OK)

FIGURE 9.12 The Move Pages dialog box lets you move a range of pages within a layout.

You can also move pages by dragging page icons in the Page Layout palette. Select the page or pages you want to move, then drag the pages to a different location beside or below other pages.

TIP: **A WORD OF CAUTION ABOUT ADDING, DELETING, AND MOVING PAGES**

Although it's possible and fairly easy to rearrange the pages in a layout by dragging page icons in the Page Layout palette, you should be careful about doing so for a couple of reasons: 1) The result of moving pages—especially multiple, nonsequential pages—is hard to anticipate, and 2) the Undo command (Edit menu) is not available after you drag page icons in the Page Layout palette. It's often safer to cut or copy items from one page and then paste them onto another page rather than move a page.

Applying a master page to layout pages

When you add new pages to a layout you can base them on any of the layout's master pages or you can add blank pages. If you subsequently change your mind, you can assign a different master page to any layout page. To change the master page that's applied to a layout page, click a master page icon in the Page Layout palette, and then drag the pointer onto a layout page. When the layout page is highlighted, release the mouse button. You can apply only one master page at a time to a layout page.

In addition to the named master pages that are listed in the top portion of the Page Layout palette, all layouts include a blank single page master, and facing-page layouts also have a blank facing-page master. Blank masters are often used as placeholders for full-page ads or as temporary placeholders for undesigned layout pages.

Numbering pages

One of the most common elements on the master pages of multipage publications is a page number—or rather a special character that automatically assigns the correct page number to all pages in the layout that are based on that master page. Generally, all of the master pages in a layout will have identical page numbers, which ensures that the formatting of page numbers on all layout pages will be the same.

Although it's possible to assign page numbers manually to every page in a layout, it's a poor approach. If you did, adding or deleting a page would require manually renumbering all subsequent pages. The correct way to accomplish page numbering is via master pages. To set up automatic page numbering:

1. Open the Page Layout palette (Window > Page Layout), and then display the layout's master page by double-clicking its icon in the upper part of the palette.

2. Create a text box to contain the page number and position it on the page where you want the page number to appear. If you are working on a facing-page master page, you must add a text box to the left (verso) component of the page and the right (recto) component of the page, and they should be mirror images of each other. (Note: Page numbers are usually placed outside the margin guides near the outside edge of the page and away from the spine.)

   If the layout has or will eventually have multiple master pages, you can configure the page number on one master page, and then copy the text box and paste it onto other master pages. (Choose Edit > Paste in Place to place the copied text box in the same location as the original text box.)

3. With the cursor flashing in the text box you created, press Command+3 (Mac) or Control +3 (Windows) to insert the automatic page number character (<#>).

4. Highlight the automatic page number character, and then modify its formatting—by changing the font, size, alignment, and so on—until it looks the way you want your page numbers to look.

To make sure that the automatic page number character is working correctly, display a layout page that's based on the master page you just modified (by double-clicking a layout page in the Page Layout palette). The correct page number should appear in a text box that's identical to the one on the master page. If the correct page number is not displayed, return to the master page and make sure you've correctly followed the steps above.

Dividing a layout into sections

After you set up automatic page numbering for a layout, the pages are numbered sequentially starting with page 1; however, you may want to use different page numbering schemes for different portions of a publication. For example, you might want to assign roman numerals to the first several pages of a layout, and then switch to standard numbers for the remaining pages. You accomplish this by dividing the layout into two independently numbered sections.

Any page in a layout can begin a new section, and a section—with its own page numbering scheme—continues until you reach a page that begins a new section. A layout can include as many sections as you want. To create a section:

1. In the Page Layout palette (Window > Page Layout), click the page you want to designate as the start of section.

2. Choose Page > Section.

3. In the Section dialog box (**Figure 9.13**), check Section Start.

4. Use the controls in the Page Numbering section to configure page numbering. You can assign a prefix (or not), specify the first page number in the section, and choose one of five formats.

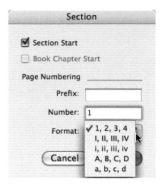

FIGURE 9.13 When you start a section, you can specify the number of the page and the format. Here you see the five available format options.

TIP: ***STARTING A LAYOUT ON A VERSO PAGE***

You can begin a layout on a verso (left) page by dragging a master page icon or a layout page icon to the left of page 1 in the Page Layout palette. If you do this, you'll probably want to designate the first page as the start of a section so that you can assign it an even number in the Section dialog box.

Using layers

Each item on a page occupies a single level in the page's stacking order, and you can use the Send Backward/Send to Back and Bring Forward/Bring to Front commands (Item menu) to change an item's position in the stacking order. You can also use layers to organize the items on pages. (For more information about changing the stacking order of items, see Chapter 3.)

A layer is a collection of items with its own stacking order. The items on each layer are in front of and obscure the items on all lower layers. You can arrange the layers in a layout by moving them up or down relative to other layers, and you can show or hide and enable or disable output for layers.

Layers aren't very useful for simple layouts with relatively few items, but they can be extremely helpful for more complex layouts with many items, as well as for creating variations of a publication. For example, a simple way to get started with layers is to create one layer for text elements and a second layer for graphic elements. Or you can create two text layers for a publication that will be printed in two languages: one layer for English text and another layer for a different language, say, Spanish. If you create regional publications, you can create a layer that contains region-specific content for each region.

To create a layer:

1. Choose Window > Layers to display the Layers palette if it's not already open.

2. Choose New Layer from the Layers palette menu.

3. To name and configure the attributes of the new layer, double-click it in the list.

4. Use the controls in the Attributes dialog box (**Figure 9.14**) to configure the layer. Check Visible to display the layer; check Suppress Printout to omit the layer when printing; check Locked to prevent changes to items on the layer; and check Keep Runaround to wrap text around items on the layer when the layer is hidden.

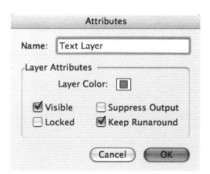

FIGURE 9.14 The controls in the Attributes dialog box let you configure several layer attributes.

Managing layers

The Layers palette (**Figure 9.15**) displays a list of the layers in a layout. The palette menu offers several commands for managing, displaying, and locking layers.

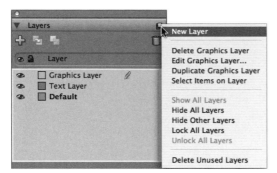

FIGURE 9.15 The Layers palette displays a list of the layers in a layout. The pencil icon is displayed to the right of the currently active layer.

The top layer in the list is the frontmost layer in the layout, and the items on this layer are in front of items on all other layers. The same is true for each successively lower layer. You can move a layer by clicking and dragging it vertically.

Click the eye icon 👁 to the left of a layer to hide the layer; click again to show the layer. Click the lock icon 🔒 to the left of a layer to prevent changes to items on the layer; click again to unlock the layer. If you double-click a layer, the Attributes dialog box is displayed and you can change the settings as needed.

To delete a layer, select it in the list, and then click the trash can at the top-right of the Layers palette or choose Delete [Name of Layer} Layer from the palette menu.

Moving items between layers

Each time you create a new item, it's placed on the currently active layer, which is indicated in the Layers palette by the Pencil icon ✏. To move a selected item to a different layer, click the item icon ⠿ in the Layers palette and drag it vertically to a different layer.

CHAPTER 10

Print

MOST PUBLICATIONS ARE PRINTED SEVERAL TIMES prior to final output. In the early stages of a workflow, black-and-white "roughs" can be useful for editorial and design markup. As decisions are made and details added, color proofs printed at various stages provide a more accurate, hands-on preview of the final piece. Color publications that are bound for a printing press ultimately need to be output as color separations. QuarkXPress has a versatile set of printing tools that enables you to output any kind of print layout on virtually any type of printer.

In this chapter you'll learn how to make sure a document is ready to print, how to print black-and-white and color proofs, and how to gather all of the files required to print a layout so that you can hand them off to a print service provider. You'll also learn how print output styles can save time and ensure consistency if you use multiple printers.

Preparing to print

Printing a layout doesn't take much preparation. In fact, if you've set up your printers correctly and they're turned on and connected, you can print a layout immediately after you create it.

Here are a few things you can do before you print a layout to make sure you get what you want and don't encounter any problems.

- If guides, page grids, or text box grids are displayed, choose View > Guides, View > Page Grids, or View Text Box Grids to hide them. Deselect all items by clicking on an empty area of a page or the pasteboard. This will give you something akin to a print preview. Choose View > Actual Size if you want to view the layout using its true dimensions. (Note: Depending on the size of your monitor's pixels and the configuration of your monitor, Actual Size may not be 100% accurate.)

- To "soft proof" a layout onscreen, choose View > Proof Output, and then choose an output option from the submenu. When you choose an option, QuarkXPress uses the information in the source setup, output setup, and any color profiles assigned to imported pictures to simulate onscreen how the layout will look when printed. (See Chapter 8 for information about color management and color source and output setups.)

- Check to make sure all imported pictures are available and up-to-date. When you print a layout, QuarkXPress sends the original graphic files for all imported pictures to the printer. To do this, QuarkXPress stores the name of each imported graphic and the path to each file within the project file. If you move, delete, or rename a graphic file, it will not be available for printing. If this occurs, you'll receive a warning when you print with the option to find the file or print without it and use a low-resolution version of the graphic instead.

To check the status of the pictures in a layout:

1. Choose Utilities > Usage.

2. Click Pictures in the scroll list on the left side of the Usage for [Name of Layout] dialog box (**Figure 10.1**). All pictures in the layout are displayed in the Pictures section. If "OK" is displayed in the Status column, it means that the original picture file is available. "Missing" means that the file is no longer in its original location (it may have been deleted, moved, or renamed). "Modified"

means that the original file is available but it has been resaved—and perhaps modified—since it was originally imported.

3. To correct a modified graphic, select it in the list, and then click the Update button. To correct a missing graphic, click the Update button, and then locate and select the correct file. If the graphic has been modified since it was imported, the status will change from Missing to Modified. Click Update again to update the file.

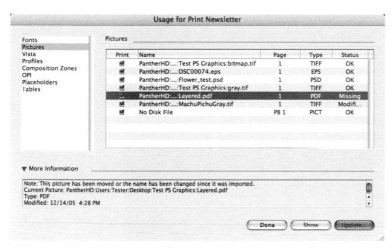

FIGURE 10.1 The Pictures pane of the Usage dialog box lists all pictures in a layout and displays their current status: OK, Missing, or Modified. The check boxes to the left of picture names let you print individual pictures or prevent them from printing.

When a picture is selected, information about the picture and its status is displayed in the More Information area. Clicking the triangle next to More Information alternately hides and shows information. If you click the Show button, the currently selected picture is displayed in the project window. Click the other options in the scroll list on the left side of the Usage dialog box, including Fonts, Composition Zones, and Tables, to display information about other elements in the layout.

A Job Jacket is a comprehensive set of specifications that define a print (or Web) layout. Assigning a Job Jacket to a layout ensures that the layout adheres to the specifications in the Job Jacket. For example, if a Job Jacket specifies that a layout can use only CMYK colors, any layout to which the Job Jacket is assigned will be limited to CMYK colors. Although using Job Jackets can be an effective way to ensure that layouts adhere to a predefined set of job specifications, using them is not easy. Check with your service provider to see if implementing Job Jackets would benefit your work site.

The Print dialog box

When you're ready to print a layout, choose File > Print. The Print dialog box (**Figure 10.2**) is displayed. The controls in the bottom portion of the Print dialog box change depending on the option selected in the list on the left; the controls in the top portion of the dialog box are always available.

Choose a printer from the Printer menu and, if you've created any, a print output style from the Print Style menu. (Print output styles are explained later in this chapter.) Use the other controls at the top of the dialog box to specify how many pages you want to print, the number of copies, and so on. In the Preview area at the upper-right corner, a blue rectangle indicates the edge of the printed page, the green rectangle shows the imageable area on the paper, and the black rectangle indicates the edge of the paper.

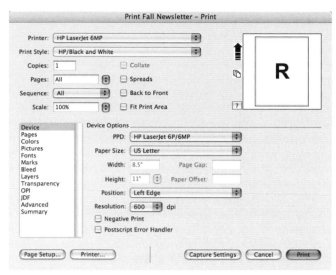

FIGURE 10.2 The Print dialog box. The controls at the top of the dialog box are always available; the controls displayed at the bottom of the dialog box depend on the currently selected printer and print style. This screen shot shows the Device controls.

TIP: **PRINTING NONSEQUENTIAL PAGES**

The Pages field in the Print dialog box lets you print a specific page (for example, 3), a range of pages (3-8), nonsequential pages (1, 3, 6), or any combination of specific pages and page ranges (1, 2-4, 6).

You shouldn't have to make many changes in the various panes of the Print dialog box, but if you have a print job with special requirements, QuarkXPress offers many options for controlling how a layout is printed. The controls available depend on the selected printer and print style. Here's a brief description of each of the panes in the Print dialog box.

- **Device pane:** When available, the PPD menu lets you select a printer description (which should match the selected printer). The remaining controls let you specify printer-specific options such as paper size and resolution.

- **Pages pane:** Offers page-specific controls including orientation, flipping, printing thumbnails, and tiling (printing large layouts in multiple, paper-size sections).

- **Colors pane:** Lets you control how colors are printed. For some printers, the Mode menu lets you choose between Composite and Separations. The Setup menu lets you choose an output setup. (See Chapter 8 for information about output setups.) Output colors are listed with the option to print or not print individual colors and control halftone options for individual colors.

- **Pictures pane:** The Output menu lets you choose a print resolution for pictures. Normal prints pictures at the highest possible resolution by using the original graphic files. Low Resolution prints pictures using a low-resolution screen preview. Rough omits pictures from the printed page and replaces them with Xs that indicate the position of picture boxes.

- **Fonts pane:** Lets you control what fonts are sent to the printer.

- **Marks pane:** Lets you add registration, crop, and bleed marks and specify the size of crop marks and the distance of crop marks from the edge of the page.

- **Bleed pane:** Provides controls for specifying how bleed items (that is, items that extend beyond the trimmed edge of the page) are printed. If you choose Symmetric or Asymmetric from the Bleed Type menu, you can specify the amount of bleed (that is, the distance from the trimmed page edge to the edge of the printed area).

- **Layers pane:** Lets you print all layers or only selected layers and displays a list of colors used in each layer. (See Chapter 9 for more information about layers.)

- **Transparency pane:** Provides controls for specifying the output resolution of drop shadows, items to which opacity has been applied, and items with blended backgrounds.

- **OPI pane:** Provides a handful of controls for using an Open Prepress Interface (OPI) server, which replaces low-resolution graphic files with high-resolution versions during output.

- **JDF pane:** Provides the option to save a JDF (Job Definition Format) file based on the project's Job Jacket structure.

- **Advanced pane:** Has a menu that lets you choose between PostScript Level 2 and Level 3. Check your printer specifications to see what level it supports.

- **Summary pane:** Displays a summary of the settings in most of the other panes.

After you've finished specifying print settings, click Print to send the layout to the selected printer. A status window is displayed as the layout prints and shows information about what's being printed and the overall progress.

If you click the Capture Settings button in the Print dialog box, the dialog box closes and the current settings in all panes are saved until the next time you print a layout. If you intend to use captured settings frequently, create a print output style (see next topic).

Using print output styles

Given the intimidating number of controls in the Print dialog box, not to mention the huge number of printer models in the world, it's fortunate that QuarkXPress offers a way to automate the print process. The solution is print output styles. Like paragraph and character style sheets, which let you quickly and consistently format text, print output styles let you print layouts using a set of predefined output specifications.

You could, for example, create a print output style for printing grayscale proofs with your low-resolution black-and-white printer and another one for printing medium-resolution color proofs to your color laser printer. Each time you print, you simply choose the appropriate printer output style and minimize the number of steps required to do the job.

Like paragraph and character style sheets, you must create a print output style before you can use it to print a layout. To create a print output style:

1. Choose Edit > Output Styles.

2. In the Output Styles dialog box, click New and choose Print from the menu.

3. In the Edit Print Style dialog box (**Figure 10.3**), enter a name in the Print Style field.

4. In the Device pane, select a PPD for the printer you intend to use, and then modify the settings in the various panes according to your output requirements.

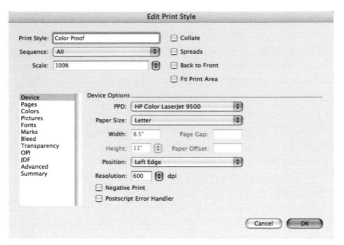

FIGURE 10.3 The Edit Print Style dialog box is much like the Print dialog box.

You can also create a print output style using the Print dialog box. To do so, modify the settings in the various panes to suit your requirements, and then choose New Print Output Style from the Print Style menu.

After you create a print output style, it's displayed in the Print Style menu in the Print dialog box and you can choose it when you need to print to a specific printer using the settings in the print output style. If you choose a custom print output style, make sure to select the correct output device from the Printer menu.

> TIP: **OUTPUT STYLES FOR LAYOUTS EXPORTED AS PDF AND EPS**
>
> *In addition to print output styles, you can create output styles for exported PDF files and exported EPS files. To create a PDF output style, click the New button in the Output Styles dialog box and choose PDF; choose EPS to create an EPS output style. To export a layout as PDF or EPS, choose File > Export > Layout as PDF or Layout as EPS. (See Chapter 11 for more information about exporting PDF files.)*

Printing drafts

As a print publication moves through its life cycle, you're probably going to want to print a number of preliminary versions before it's ready for final output. Especially in the early stages, it may not be necessary—or economical given the generally high price of consumables for color printers—to print high-quality color proofs. For example, if you need to print a rough early draft, perhaps for editorial review and markup, you can reduce printing time and the cost of consumables by printing low-resolution grayscale pages. Here are a few other suggestions for printing early drafts:

- If the highest possible resolution isn't necessary, choose the lowest resolution available in the Resolution menu of the Device pane.

- To save paper, make sure Include Blank Pages isn't checked in the Pages pane.

- To print grayscale—especially to a color printer to save ink—choose Mode > Composite and Setup > Grayscale in the Color pane.

- Choose Low Resolution in the Output menu of the Pictures pane to speed printing but reduce image clarity; choose Rough to replace pictures with Xs that indicate the boundary of picture boxes and further reduce print time.

- If a layout includes layers, select only the ones you want to print in the Layers pane.

- Check Thumbnails in the Pages pane to print reduced-sized versions of pages on a single sheet of paper.

Most important of all, if you intend to print rough drafts regularly using the same printer and print specifications, you should create a print output style.

Printing color proofs

Printing color proofs is pretty much the same as printing rough drafts, with perhaps a few tweaks in the Print dialog box. To print color proofs:

- For the best-possible overall clarity, choose or enter the highest possible resolution from the Resolution menu in the Device pane. To reduce printing time as well as clarity, lower the resolution.

- In the Colors pane, choose Mode > Composite and Setup > Composite CMYK if you're printing to a four-color inkjet or laser printer.

Again, the best solution for printing color proofs is to create a print output style with the appropriate settings and use it when needed.

Collecting files for final output

If your layouts will ultimately be printed on a printing press, you'll probably hand off your finished QuarkXPress project files to a print service provider when layouts are ready for final output. If you intend to send QuarkXPress project files to your service provider, you must include the original image files for all imported pictures, as well as all font files. If you don't include picture files, low-resolution versions will be used instead, and if you don't include font files, there's no guarantee that your provider can replace them.

Manually gathering all of the files required to print a design-intensive publication could take a considerable amount of time, plus there's a real possibility of failing to include a required file. Fortunately, there's a better way. The Collect for Output command (File menu) automates the task of gathering all files required to print a layout. When you're ready to send a layout to your service provider:

1. Make sure the layout is ready for final output, and then choose File > Collect for Output.

2. In the Collect for Output dialog box (**Figure 10.4**), select the folder in which collected files will be placed or click the New Folder button to create a new one.

3. In the Save As field, enter a name for the report that's included in the collection of files. The report is a text file that contains information about the layout.

4. In the Collect for Output section at the bottom of the dialog box, check the files you want to collect. It's safest to collect all files, especially if you're not sure what files your service provider needs. (Note: If you collect fonts, QuarkXPress will attempt to collect fonts within imported EPS files, as well as fonts used in the layout.)

5. Optional: In the Vista section, check Render Picture Attributes to apply effects to picture files prior to collecting them.

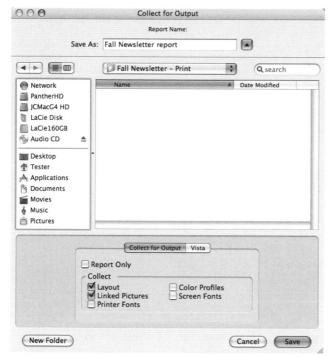

FIGURE 10.4 The Collect for Output dialog box lets you choose or create a collection folder and choose what files to collect.

After you collect files for output you should check the folder that contains the files to make sure everything is in order. **Figure 10.5** shows the contents of a typical folder. If you collect all files, a QuarkXPress project file and the report are placed within the collection folder; the Fonts, Pictures, and Profiles folders contain the other types of files. (Note: If you choose Collect for Output for a project that contains multiple layouts, the QuarkXPress project file that's generated contains only the active layout.)

If the collection folder contains the required files, it's ready to be handed off to your service provider. A word of caution at this point: If you checked Layout in the Collect for Output dialog box, you now have two copies of the layout: the one in the project file that's still displayed onscreen and the copy that's placed in the collection folder. If you subsequently discover that changes need to be made to the layout, you need to make sure they're made to both versions of the layout. Or you can simply deem one copy (the onsite version or the version you sent to your service provider) as the current version, update it, and then replace the other version.

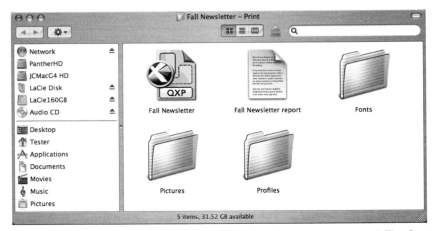

FIGURE 10.5 This folder was created using the Collect for Output command. The QuarkXPress project file contains a print layout; the report is a text file that contains information about the layout, such as fonts used. The three folders contain other types of collected files.

You can also create a PDF output style using the PDF Export Options dialog box. To do so, modify the settings in the various panes to suit your requirements, and then choose New PDF Output Style from the PDF Style menu.

After you name and save the PDF output style, it's listed in the PDF Style menu with the default styles and you can choose it when you export a layout as PDF.

CHAPTER 11

PDF

OVER THE PAST DECADE, Portable Document Format (PDF) files have become commonplace and invaluable in print and Web publishing. In the print world, PDF files have a broad range of uses—from electronic markup and review to printing everything from proofs to high-resolution color separations for off-set printing to electronic document archiving. You can also create PDF files that are intended to be displayed on a monitor rather than printed with the option to include PDF-specific elements such as hyperlinks and bookmarks.

In this chapter you'll learn how to specify PDF export preferences and how to export PDF files.

Planning layouts for PDF

It's important to mention up front that the option to export a layout as PDF is available only for print layouts. Although most print layouts are ultimately printed, it's also possible to create print layouts that will be exported as PDF for viewing onscreen.

If you're creating a layout that will be distributed in print form (a magazine layout or a newsletter, for instance), you don't have to worry about the implications of exporting the layout as PDF until you need to create a PDF for review or output. If, on the other hand, you're creating a layout whose primary purpose is to be viewed onscreen, you'll need to take a slightly different approach in setting it up than for printed publications. For example, it's a good idea to base the page dimensions (in the New Layout dialog box) on a standard monitor size, and you should avoid creating a facing-page layout because you can't fold a monitor in half.

Setting PDF Preferences

You don't have to change any of the PDF-related settings in the PDF pane of the Preferences dialog box (**Figure 11.1**), but it's helpful to know what options are available.

- If Direct to PDF is selected, QuarkXPress will generate a PDF file when you export a layout as PDF, and you have the option to log errors and choose a log folder.

- If Create PostScript File for Later Distilling is selected, QuarkXPress will create a PostScript file when you export a layout as PDF. You will need a third-party distilling tool (such as Acrobat Distiller) to convert PostScript files into PDF files. If you choose to create PostScript files, you can use the associated controls to choose a Watched folder where the PostScript files are stored—presumably to be automatically converted to PDF by a third-party program that is "watching" the folder—or you can use the default Watched folder.

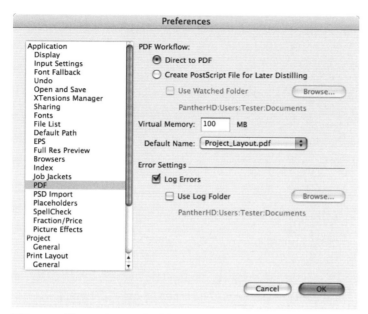

FIGURE 11.1 The settings in the PDF pane of the Preferences dialog box determine what occurs when you export a layout as PDF.

Any changes you make to PDF preferences are applied to the current project. If no projects are open, the settings are used for all new projects, although of course you can change them later.

Exporting layouts as PDF

When you're ready to export a layout as PDF, do the following:

1. Choose File > Export > Layout as PDF or click the Export button at the bottom of the project window, and then choose Layout as PDF from the submenu.

2. From the Export as PDF dialog box (**Figure 11.2**), select the folder where you want to save the PDF file or click New Folder to create a new one.

3. In the Pages field, specify the pages you want to export or choose All from the menu to export all pages in the layout.

4. Choose a PDF export style from the PDF Style menu. The menu offers seven default PDF output styles:

- **Screen - Low Quality/Low Resolution or Screen - Medium Quality/Medium Resolution:** Both of these options export color and grayscale images at 72 dpi and are appropriate for onscreen display, electronic markup and review, and printing low-resolution proofs.

- **Print - Medium Quality/Medium Resolution:** Exports color and grayscale images at 150 dpi and is appropriate for medium-resolution proof printing.

- **Press - High Quality/High Resolution:** Exports color and grayscale images at 300 dpi and is appropriate for printing color separations for use in off-set printing.

- **PDF/X-1a:2001 or PDF/X3:2002:** Both are subsets of the standard PDF format designed specifically for reliable prepress data exchange. PDF/X-1a files include only CMYK colors and named spot colors and no RGB colors or device independent (color-managed) information. PDF/X3 allows the inclusion of other color models (for example, RGB and Lab) with color profiles attached.

- **Default PDF Output Style:** Exports color and grayscale graphics at 72 dpi and is appropriate for onscreen display, electronic markup and review, and printing low-resolution proofs.

FIGURE 11.2 Unless you have special requirements, creating a PDF is a simple matter of choosing a PDF Style and clicking Save. If you click Options, you can customize the settings of the PDF you're exporting.

5. Optional: Click Options to display the PDF Export Options for [Name of Layout] dialog box (**Figure 11.3**). This dialog box contains 13 panes. Collectively, these panes offer dozens of choices for configuring a PDF file. If you've selected a PDF preset, there's no need to modify any of the settings in this dialog box; however, if you have specialized requirements, you can change the settings as needed. Here's a brief description of each pane:

- **Pages:** Lets you export facing pages as spreads and export each page as a separate PDF file. Also provides the option to include or exclude blank pages and to embed color or black-and-white thumbnails of pages.

- **Meta Data:** Provides four fields for adding meta data to a PDF file: Title, Subject, Author, and Keywords.

- **Hyperlinks:** If the layout you're exporting contains hyperlinks, you can include them in the exported PDF by checking Include Hyperlinks in this pane. You also have the option to export lists and indexes as hyperlinks and to export all lists or a specific list as bookmarks. Appearance controls let you specify how hyperlinks are displayed.

- **Compression:** Lets you choose a compression method and specify a resolution for color, grayscale, and monochrome images.

- **Color:** Includes controls for printing composite color or color separations with the option to include or exclude individual colors.

- **Fonts:** Lets you embed all fonts used in the layout or only selected fonts.

- **Marks:** Provides the option to include registration marks and specify their placement and the option to include bleed marks.

- **Bleed:** Lets you specify how bleed items (items that extend beyond the page's trimline) are handled in the PDF file.

- **Layers:** Allows you to include all layers in the layout or any subset of layers.

- **Transparency:** Allows you to assign an output resolution independently to vector images, blends, and drop shadow.

- **OPI:** Lets you enable or disable Open Prepress Interface (OPI). When enabled, you can replace low-resolution images with high-resolution versions.

- **JDF:** Provides the option to create a Job Definition Format file in the exported PDF file.

- **Summary:** Displays a summary of the settings in most of the panes in the dialog box.

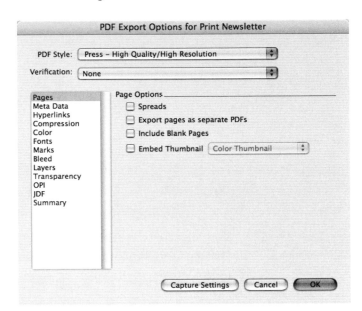

FIGURE 11.3 The PDF Export Options dialog box includes 13 panes and many controls for configuring PDF files. This screen shot shows the controls in the Pages pane.

If you make changes in the PDF Export Options dialog box, clicking the Capture Settings button will close the dialog box and save any changes you've made. The next time you export a layout as PDF, the settings you captured are used to export the PDF.

TIP: **CREATING PDFS USING THE PRINT DIALOG BOX**

If you use the Mac version of QuarkXPress, you can create PDF files using the Print dialog box. To do so, choose File > Print, and then click the Printer button at the bottom of the Print [Name of Layout] dialog box. In the Print dialog box, click the PDF button in the lower-left corner, and then choose one of the options from the menu.

After you export a PDF layout, the file can be opened and printed using Adobe Acrobat Professional, Adobe Reader, or (on a Mac) Preview. If you need to modify a PDF file, you'll need a PDF-editing program. Several commercial and free PDF editors are available.

Using PDF Output Styles

If none of the default PDF output styles is appropriate for your needs, you can create custom PDF output styles. To create a PDF output style:

1. Choose Edit > Output Styles.

2. In the Output Styles dialog box, click New and choose PDF from the menu.

3. In the Edit PDF Styles dialog box (**Figure 11.4**), enter a name in the PDF Style field.

4. Modify the settings in the various panes based on how the PDF will be used.

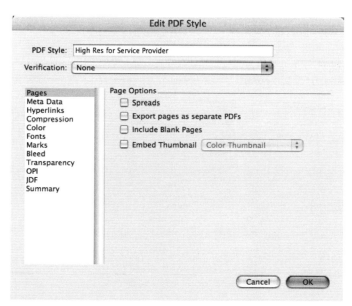

FIGURE 11.4 The Edit PDF Style dialog box is much like the PDF Export Options dialog box.

You can also create a PDF output style using the PDF Export Options dialog box (File > Layout as PDF > Options). To do so, modify the settings in the various panes of the dialog box to suit your requirements, and then choose New PDF Output Style from the PDF Style menu. After you create a PDF output style, it's listed in the PDF Style menu in the Export as PDF dialog box along with the default PDF output styles, and you can choose it when you export a layout as PDF.

CHAPTER 12

Web

WHEN QUARKXPRESS 1 WAS RELEASED IN 1987, print publishing was the only kind of publishing. This would change during the 1990s with the growth of the Internet and the advent of Web publishing. One result of these developments was that many print publishing companies suddenly needed software tools that allowed them to repurpose their print content on the Web and build Web pages. Quark's answer was to add Web publishing features to QuarkXPress 5. This gave existing users a familiar environment for building Web pages and enabled all users—new and old—to publish for both print and the Web.

In this chapter you'll learn to create Web layouts and how to add a wide range of elements to a Web layout, including text, pictures, hyperlinks, menus, and image maps. You'll also learn how to preview and export Web layouts and how to convert layouts between print and Web.

Planning and designing Web layouts

One of the major advantages of being able to create Web layouts with QuarkXPress is that the process of laying out a page in a Web layout is much the same as in a print layout. You add text, picture, and no-content boxes, lines, text on a path, and tables—the same items you add to printed pages. The two main differences between Web pages and print pages are: 1) Web pages can include many types of items that aren't possible on printed pages—video, sound, animations, hyperlinks, buttons, and so on; and 2) HTML files do not support many features that are available for print publications, such as justified alignment, kerning and tracking, and nonrectangular text boxes, to mention only a few. This is true regardless of whether you use QuarkXPress or another desktop publishing program.

Another significant difference between Web layouts and print layouts is the meaning of the term "page." Printed publications have a specific page size and begin with page 1, and the pages continue sequentially until the last page. This isn't true of Web publications. A Web page doesn't require a fixed page size. Pages aren't numbered sequentially, although they're often set up in a traditional sequence; you can't turn a page to navigate to the next one (instead, you often click on an icon or a teaser line of text); and there is no "last" page. The Web frees readers to jump around at will via hyperlinks.

Although the tools QuarkXPress provides for creating Web and print layouts are the same in many ways, Web publications are very different than print publications and creating them requires a different mind-set. How you use QuarkXPress's Web publishing features will depend on your needs. For example, you can create a project that contains a single Web layout that, when exported, becomes a simple Web site—with a home page and additional pages that a viewer can access via the home page. Or you can simultaneously create a print publication and a Web publication in a single project with one print layout and one Web layout. Once exported, the Web layout could be a stand-alone Web site or part of a larger site.

This chapter focuses on the nuts and bolts of building a Web layout and concludes with an explanation of how to export Web layouts as HTML files. How you ultimately use these HTML files at your site depends on many factors and is beyond the scope of this book.

Master pages in Web layouts are the same as for print layouts. Although it's possi-ble to automatically place page numbers on the pages in a Web layout, Web pages usually don't include them. Many Web sites provide the same set of navigation con-trols in the same place on every page—for instance, a table of contents. These types of elements are appropriate to place on the master page of a Web layout.

Creating a Web layout

You have two options for creating a Web layout from scratch:

- When you create a new project file (File > New Project), choosing Web from the Layout Type menu in the New Project dialog box displays a set of controls for specifying a variety of layout-wide settings. When you click OK to close the dia-log box, the new project contains a single Web layout. You can then add more layouts—print, Web, or interactive—as needed by choosing Layout > New.

- You can add a new Web layout to an existing project by choosing Layout > New, and then choosing Web from the Layout Type menu in the New Layout dialog box (**Figure 12.1**). If you choose to create a Web layout in the New Project dialog box, the controls are essentially the same as those in the New Layout dialog box if Web is the selected layout type.

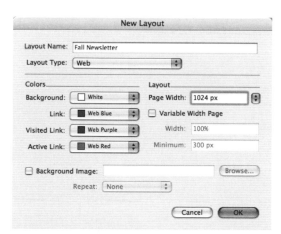

FIGURE 12.1 When you create a Web layout, the options in the New Layout dialog box let you specify several default settings for the layout, including the color used for page backgrounds and hyperlinks and the width of the page.

A few things to note about the options in the New Project/New Layout dialog boxes when you choose to create a Web layout:

- The default settings for color are standard. You can choose a different color from the list or choose New to create a custom color.

- In the Layout section, specify a Page Width value for a fixed width and disregard the width of the browser window. If you check Variable Width Page, the width of exported Web pages changes when a viewer changes the width of the browser window. The Width and Minimum fields are available for variable width pages. If you enter a Width value below 100%, a vertical guideline is displayed. The higher the value, the closer the guide is to the right edge of the page. The value you enter in the Minimum field determines the narrowest allowable page width (in pixels).

- If you check Background Image, you can select a picture (in .jpg, .gif, or .png format) to use as the page background. The choices in the Repeat menu let you specify if and how the image is repeated.

TIP: **COMBINING WEB AND PRINT LAYOUTS**

One of the benefits of combining a Web layout with a print layout in a single QuarkXPress project file is that you can share text and graphic elements among multiple layouts. Any change you make to shared content in one layout is automatically applied to the other layout.

After you open a Web layout, you'll notice that an additional palette is displayed on the left side of your monitor. The Web Tools palette (**Figure 12.2**) includes three tool groupings that let you add image maps and HTML form elements (for example, check boxes and radio buttons) and work with rollovers. (You'll learn more about these tools later in this chapter.)

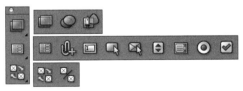

FIGURE 12.2 The Web Tools palette is displayed when a Web layout is active in the project window. The top group of three tools lets you create image maps, the middle set of nine tools lets you add form elements, and the last pair of tools lets you work with rollovers.

Working with text

When working with text in Web layouts, it's important to understand that there are several fundamental differences between text that's output with a printer and text that's displayed in a browser window on a monitor. The biggest difference is that many of QuarkXPress's high-end typographic features look great when printed but are not supported when you export Web layouts, including justified alignment, hyphenation, tabs, baseline shift, kerning and tracking, scaling, and flipping. (For a complete list of unsupported features and limitations, see the QuarkXPress Help file.)

It's worth mentioning that all of the unsupported text-formatting features are available for Web layouts; however, when you export a Web layout as an HTML file, unsupported formatting is omitted, and depending on which features you've used in the layout, the text in the resulting Web pages may look considerably different than the text in the Web layout.

QuarkXPress offers two options for handling text boxes in Web layouts.

- **Raster text boxes:** Text boxes in Web layouts have one setting that's not available for text boxes in print layouts. In Web layouts, the Convert to Graphic on Export check box in the Modify dialog box (it's available in all panes) determines how the text is handled when exported. When checked, the text in the selected box is converted to a picture when you export the layout as HTML. (You'll learn how to export layouts as HTML later in this chapter.) A camera icon 📷 is displayed in the upper-right corner of text boxes for which Convert to Graphic on Export is checked.

  The benefit of raster text boxes is that the text in an exported HTML page when displayed in a browser window looks identical to the text in the Web layout; however, pictures take longer to download than text, the text cannot be edited if the exported HTML file is opened in an HTML-editing program, and the text cannot be searched by a viewer.

- **HTML text boxes:** If you don't check Convert to Graphic on Export for a text box, the text is exported as HTML text, which has several limitations of its own. HTML text boxes are editable and searchable, but you can't be sure if the fonts used will be available on viewers' computers. If not, substitute fonts will be used instead, and they look considerably different than the originals. Unsupported features include rotation, fractional font sizes, and linking. (See the QuarkXPress Help file for a complete list of unsupported features.)

Other than the aforementioned limitations, working with text in a Web layout is the same as working with text in a print layout. Importing, highlighting, formatting, and so on are identical, but because of the number of specialized typographic features that are not supported in HTML files, it's a good idea to simplify text formatting in Web layouts as much as possible.

TIP: **VARIABLE-WIDTH TEXT BOXES**

In addition to creating fixed-width text boxes, you can create text boxes that get wider or narrower when the viewer of a Web page changes the width of the browser window. To create a variable-width text box, select a text box, and then check Make Variable Width in the Text pane of the Modify dialog box. This feature works well when used in tandem with variable width pages.

Working with pictures, lines, and other items

Importing and modifying pictures in Web layouts is the same as in print layouts, which means you can import pictures in a wide variety of formats, including formats that aren't supported in HTML pages. When you export a Web layout as HTML, pictures in formats that aren't supported in HTML pages, including .tif, .psd, and .eps, are converted into supported formats (.jpg, .gif, or .png).

In Web layouts, the Modify dialog box for all items includes an additional pane named Export (**Figure 12.3**). The settings you make in this pane determine how the picture in the selected picture box is handled when the layout is exported as HTML. The same controls are available in the Export pane of the Measurements palette (**Figure 12.4**).

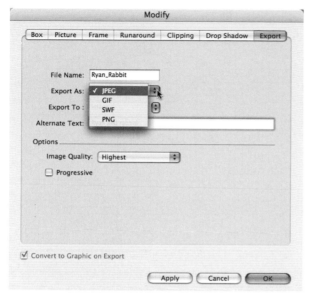

FIGURE 12.3 The Export pane of the Modify dialog box for a picture lets you choose the Web-compatible file format used to save a copy of the picture when the layout is exported as HTML. The controls in the Options area change depending on the choice you make in the Export As menu. This example shows the options that are available for JPEG pictures.

FIGURE 12.4 The Export tab of the Measurements palette offers the same controls as the Export pane of the Modify dialog box.

In addition to pictures, the following types of items are converted to pictures when you export a Web layout to HTML: lines, text on a path, no-content boxes, and empty boxes. The Export pane of the Modify dialog box and the Export tab of the Measurements palette let you control how these types of items are converted when you export the layout as HTML. **Figure 12.5** shows the controls available for text on a path. The controls are nearly identical for other types of items.

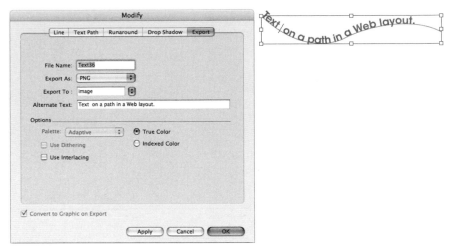

FIGURE 12.5 Because HTML does not support text on a path, text paths are converted to pictures when you export a Web layout as HTML. The Convert to Graphic on Export box is automatically selected in the Modify dialog box for all items that must be converted to pictures, and they're the same options that are available for pictures.

If a Web layout includes a table, you can either export the table as a graphic—by checking Convert Table to Graphic on Export in the Modify dialog box—or you can export it as an HTML table by unchecking Convert Table to Graphic on Export.

Adding other elements to Web layouts

One of the reasons Web publishing has grown so quickly over the past decade is that Web pages can contain much more than text, pictures, and graphic embellishments. This means that viewers of Web pages can have an interactive, multimedia experience that isn't possible with printed pages. In this section, you'll learn how to create several kinds of Web-specific items.

Hyperlinks

The ability to jump from page to page and topic to topic around the Web has been one of Internet's most seductive features, so it's nice that creating a hyperlink in a Web layout is easy. In fact, adding a hyperlink to an item in a Web layout is much the same as modifying other items: First you select the item, and then you make the required changes.

You can add a hyperlink to a text string (including text on a path), any type of box, or a line. QuarkXPress offers several methods for creating hyperlinks. Here's the easiest:

1. Highlight a range of text or select a box or a line.

2. Display the Hyperlinks (Window > Hyperlinks) palette if it's not already open (**Figure 12.6**).

3. Choose New Hyperlink from the palette menu or click the New Hyperlink button 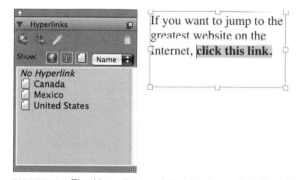 at the top-left of the palette.

4. In the New Hyperlink dialog box (**Figure 12.7**), enter a name for the hyperlink (the name is displayed in the Hyperlink palette's scroll list), and then choose an option from the Type menu. If you choose URL for a link to another site, make sure you specify a URL in the URL field. Click on the up/down arrow to display a list of URL prefixes (http://, https://, ftp://, and mailto:).

   If you choose Page, you can link to another page in the layout; if you choose Target, you can link to any anchor within the layout, if you've created any. (You can place anchors anywhere in a layout.)

FIGURE 12.6 The Hyperlinks palette displays a list of existing hyperlinks in a Web layout. In this example, a range of text is highlighted in preparation for adding a new hyperlink to it.

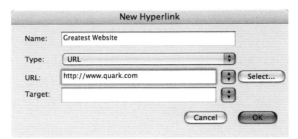

FIGURE 12.7 The New Hyperlink dialog box lets you specify what happens when a viewer of the Web page clicks the hyperlinked item.

After you create a hyperlink, it's listed in the Hyperlinks palette with the other hyperlinks in the layout. If you create a hyperlink for a text string, color and an underline are automatically added to the text—in both the layout and the exported HTML page when displayed in a browser window—to indicate that the text has a hyperlink. **Figure 12.8** shows how text to which a hyperlink has been added is displayed in QuarkXPress.

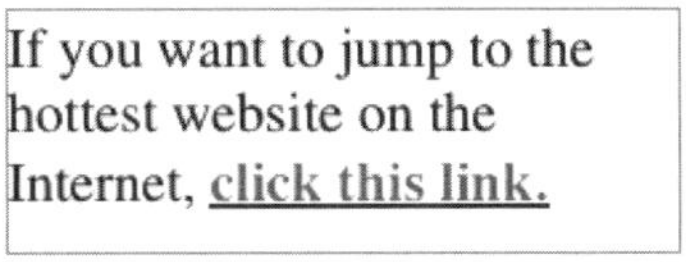

> If you want to jump to the hottest website on the Internet, click this link.

FIGURE 12.8 When you assign a hyperlink to a range of text, color and an underline are automatically added to remind you—and inform viewers of the exported Web page—that the text includes a hyperlink.

If you need to modify a hyperlink, click it in the Hyperlinks palette scroll list, and then click the Edit button at the top of the palette. To delete a hyperlink, click it in the scroll list, and then click the Trash can icon at the top of the palette or choose Delete from the palette menu. If you double-click a hyperlink in the scroll list, QuarkXPress will attempt to display the HTML page in your default Web browser. This is a good way to determine if a new hyperlink is working as intended.

Rollovers

A rollover is a picture on a Web page that changes to a different picture when a viewer moves the pointer over it. In addition to swapping pictures, the rollovers you add to your Web layouts can include a hyperlink so that when a viewer clicks the picture, the browser jumps to the assigned URL.

To create a basic rollover:

1. Select a picture box or a text box. (If you want to use a text box, you must first check Convert to Graphic on Export in the Modify dialog box. Although it's possible to use a text box for a rollover, it's not generally done.)

2. Choose Item > Basic Rollover > Create Rollover.

3. In the Rollover dialog box (**Figure 12.9**), the picture in the currently selected picture box is listed in the Default Image field. If a text box is selected, an assigned name is displayed in the Default Image field.) To choose the Rollover Image, click Select, and then locate and open the picture you want to use.

4. Optional: Enter a URL in the Hyperlink field if you want to add a hyperlink to the rollover.

Figure **12.9** The Rollover dialog box lets you choose the two images that are swapped when a viewer of the Web page moves the pointer over the selected item. You also have the option of adding a hyperlink to a rollover.

After you create a basic rollover, small icons are displayed in the upper-right corner of the selected box: The ▦ icon indicates that the box contains a pair of swappable images; the ▦ icon indicates that the box is a rollover; and the ◉ icon is displayed if the rollover includes a hyperlink.

To remove a basic rollover from a box, select the box and then choose Item > Basic Rollover > Remove Rollover. You can display each of the two pictures assigned to a rollover by choosing Item > Basic Rollover > Default Image or Item > Basic Rollover > Rollover Image.

In addition to basic rollovers, you can also create two-position rollovers. When a view of a Web page moves the pointer within a picture to which a two-position rollover has been applied, a different picture is displayed in a different box.

Image maps

An image map is a picture to which one or more hyperlinks is applied. Each hyperlink is applied to a different "hot area" within the picture. When a Web page viewer clicks a picture that includes an image map, the browser jumps to the URL assigned to the hot area in the picture within which the click occurred. For example, you could create an image map for a picture of North America so that when a viewer clicks a country, the browser jumps to a Web page with information about that country.

To create an image map:

1. Choose one of the three image map tools—Rectangle Image Map tool, Oval Image Map tool, or Bézier Image Map tool—in the Web Tools palette (**Figure 12.10**). (If the Web Tools palette is not open, choose Window > Tools > Show Web Tools.) These tools are the same as the Rectangle Box tool, the Oval Box tool, and the Bézier Pen tool with the exception that they're used to create hot areas within pictures instead of boxes. (For information about creating rectangular, oval, and Bézier boxes, see Chapter 3.)

2. Use the selected tool to create a hot area within the perimeter of a picture frame that contains a picture. (If you use the Bézier Image Map tool, you must create a closed shape.)

3. To add a hyperlink to the hot area, click the New Hyperlink button 🔍 in the Hyperlinks palette or choose New from the palette menu, and then use the controls in the New Hyperlink dialog box (Figure 12.7) to configure the hyperlink.

4. Optional: Continue to add hot spots and, if you want, hyperlinks to the picture.

FIGURE 12.10 The three image map tools in the Web Tools palette let you assign "hot areas" to pictures. Creating shapes with these tools is the same as creating boxes with the Rectangle Box tool, the Oval Box tool, and the Bézier Pen tool.

Hot areas in a Web layout are displayed only when you select a picture box that contains a picture and one or more hot areas and guides are visible (View > Guides). **Figure 12.11** shows an example of a picture box with several hot areas. If guides are not visible, you can't see, select, or modify hot areas. When the exported HTML page is displayed in a browser window, hot areas are not visible, but the arrow pointer changes to a finger pointer when the pointer is within a hot area.

FIGURE 12.11 Left: The Bézier Image Map tool was used on a map of North America to create image maps for Canada, the United States, and Mexico. The image map for the United States is selected, as indicated by the darker shade. Center: The hyperlink named "United States" is highlighted in the Hyperlinks palette to indicate that this hyperlink is assigned to the image map. Right: The Edit Hyperlink dialog box indicates that the hyperlink for the image map of the United States connects links it to another page in the Web layout named "US_Map." When a viewer of the exported Web page clicks this hot area, the US_Map page is displayed.

Hot areas in a Web layout behave much the same as boxes. You can select a hot area by clicking it with the Item tool or Picture Content tool, and you can move it or drag resizing handles to change size and shape. You can't, however, modify a hot area—for example, by applying a color or a frame—like you can modify a box.

To delete a hot area, select it with the Picture Content tool, and then press Delete or Backspace. (Don't select the hot area with the Item tool. If you do and then press Delete, you'll delete the entire picture box. If you do that by accident, simply choose Edit > Undo.) To delete all hot areas from a picture box, select the box and then choose Item > Delete All Hot Areas.

Form elements

HTML form elements allow viewers of Web pages to answer questions and provide feedback over the Internet. HTML forms have a broad range of uses—from purchasing products to collecting data to even something as simple as joining a mailing list. It's important to understand that if you intend to create Web layouts that include HTML form elements, you need to be able to handle the data received from viewers who provide information. This involves setting up a server-based system (a script or an application) that processes the form data that's received. QuarkXPress does not include this capability. For information about setting up a server-based processing system for form data, contact your Web hosting service.

The bottom group of nine tools in the Web Tools palette lets you add form elements to a Web layout. Below is brief description of each tool.

- Form Box tool ▦: This tool is a little different than the tools below in that it creates container boxes for form elements. The rest of the tools let you place a variety of elements within a form box. (All form elements must be contained within a form box.) The Form pane in the Modify dialog box (**Figure 12.12**) includes a set of controls that determine how the data from the elements within the form is handled. (Ask your Web hosting service for information about how to configure the settings in this dialog box.)

FIGURE 12.12 All HTML form elements must be contained with a form box. Here you see the Form pane of the Modify dialog box for a form box. Check with your Web hosting service about how to configure the settings in this dialog box so that the sent data is handled correctly when it's received.

The eight tools that follow let you create form elements.

- **File Selection tool** ⬛: Adds a field and an accompanying Browse button that lets a viewer of the Web page select a local file that will be uploaded when the form is submitted. **Figure 12.13** shows what a file selection control looks like in a Web layout and in a Web page.

FIGURE 12.13 Left: A file selection box in a Web layout. Right: The same element displayed in a browser window.

- **Text Field tool** ⬛: Adds a text field into which a viewer of the Web page can enter plain text (**Figure 12.14**). Use the Text Context tool to enter default text into the field.

FIGURE 12.14 Left: A text field in a Web layout. Right: The same element displayed in a browser window.

- Button tool ▣: Lets you create two different kinds of buttons: Reset and Submit (**Figure 12.15**). When a viewer clicks a Reset button, all fields and buttons in a form are returned to their default settings. When a viewer clicks a Submit button, the form data is sent according to the settings applied to the form box that contains the button. The Type menu in the Form pane of the Modify dialog box lets you choose between Reset and Submit. You can add text to a button by clicking it with the Text Content tool and then entering text.

FIGURE 12.15 Left: Reset and Submit buttons in a Web layout. Right: The same elements displayed in a browser window.

- Image Button tool ▣: Lets you use a picture as a Submit button. After you create an image button, choose File > Import to place a picture within it.

- Pop-Up Menu tool ▣ and List Box tool ▤: Both of these tools let you create pop-up menus and scrollable lists from which a viewer can choose a selection. These tools are essentially interchangeable because you can change a pop-up menu to a scroll list and vice versa. When you select a pop-up menu or a scroll list, the Type menu in the Form pane of the Modify dialog box lets you choose Pop-up Menu or List. **Figure 12.16** shows both types.

FIGURE 12.16 The pair on the left show what a pop-up menu look like in a Web layout and a browser window. The pair on the right are examples of a list box.

- Radio Button tool ◉: Lets you create a group of circular buttons from which a user can make a single selection (**Figure 12.17**). When a viewer of the Web page clicks a radio button, the previously selected button is deselected. Each button in a group must have the same group name. The Group field in the Form pane of the Modify dialog box lets you assign a group name to individual radio buttons. Click a radio button with the Text Content tool to add text to the button. (Click to the left of a button to place the text on the left side of the button; click to the right of a button to place text on the right side.)

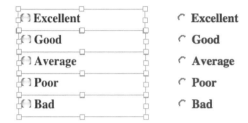

◌ Excellent	⊂ **Excellent**
◌ Good	⊂ **Good**
◌ Average	⊂ **Average**
◌ Poor	⊂ **Poor**
◌ Bad	⊂ **Bad**

FIGURE 12.17 Left: A group of radio buttons in a Web layout. Right: The same elements displayed in a browser window.

- Check Box tool ☑: Lets you create boxes that a viewer of the Web page can either check or uncheck (**Figure 12.18**). The Form pane in the Modify dialog box lets you change a check box to a radio button and vice versa.

☑ Yes, please sign me up for this special offer.   ☑ Yes, please sign me up for this special offer.

FIGURE 12.18 Left: A check box in a Web layout. Right: The same element displayed in a browser window.

TIP: **STANDARD MENUS AND CASCADING MENUS**

You can create two kinds of menus for a Web layout. In addition to the standard HTML form pop-up menus explained above, you can also create cascading menus that remain hidden until a viewer moves the pointer over specific items. For more information about creating cascading menus, see the QuarkXPress Help file.

Creating a form

Using the form-creation tools is much like using the Rectangle Box tool. All require a simple click-and-drag. To create a form:

1. Use the Form Box tool to create a form box that will contain the form elements you will use to gather data from viewers of the Web page. You can also begin by choosing any of the other tools; however, if you create a form element without first creating a form box, a form box will automatically be

created to contain the new form element. A small icon 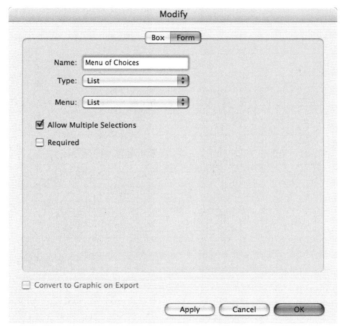 is displayed in the upper-right corner of form boxes.

2. Choose any of the eight tools that let you create form elements, and then click and drag within a form box.

3. To configure the element, choose Item > Modify, and then display the Form pane in the Modify dialog box. Each type of form element has its own set of controls. **Figure 12.19** shows the controls that are available for list boxes.

4. Optional: Choose the Text Content tool and add text to the form element. (You can add text to text fields, submit and reset buttons, and radio buttons.)

FIGURE 12.19 All HTML form elements include a set of controls that determine how the element works when a viewer uses it. This example shows the controls in the Form pane of the Modify dialog box that let you configure a list box.

Tables

Working with tables in Web layouts is much the same as in print layouts with some limitations. For example, you can't apply a drop shadow to a table in a Web layout, nor can you flip, rotate, or skew text. Dashed and striped gridlines and multiple text inset values aren't supported, either. Despite the restrictions, when viewed in a browser, tables exported as HTML usually look much the same as the original tables in the Web layouts. **Figure 12.20** shows an example.

If you want to preserve the appearance of a table when it's displayed in a Web page, check Convert Table to Graphic on Export in the Modify dialog box. If you want to preserve the appearance only of one or more cells, select a cell or a range of cells, and then check Convert Cell to Graphic on Export in the Cells pane of the Modify dialog box.

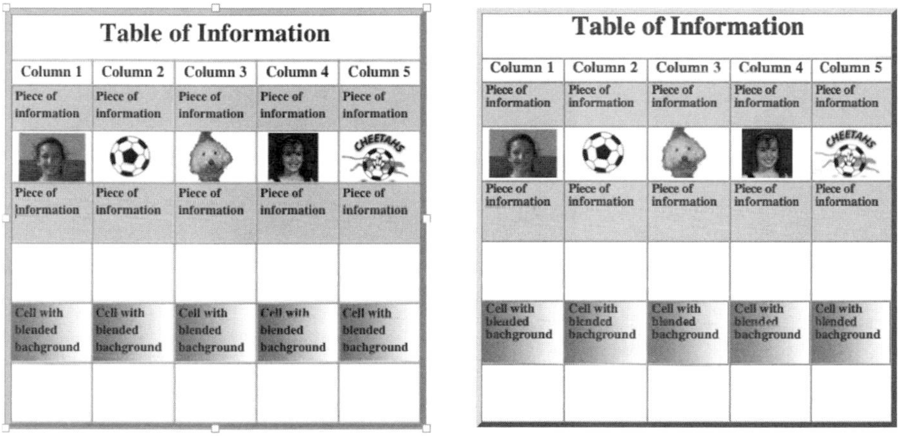

FIGURE 12.20 The screen shot on the left shows a table in a Web layout; the screen shot on the right shows the same table displayed in a browser window. Table conversion isn't exact, but generally, simple tables in Web layouts look much the same when displayed in a browser window.

Meta tags

Meta tags contain information about a Web page that's not visible in a browser window, such as a description of the page, keywords that are relevant to the page's content, author's name, and last modified date. Some search engines use meta tags for listing and ranking Web sites.

To add meta tags to a Web page, you must first create a meta tag set, and then assign the set to a page. To create a meta tag set:

1. Choose Edit > Meta Tags.

2. Click New in the Meta Tags for [Name of Project] dialog box.

3. In the Edit Meta Tag Set dialog box (**Figure 12.21**), enter a name for the meta tag set, and then click Add.

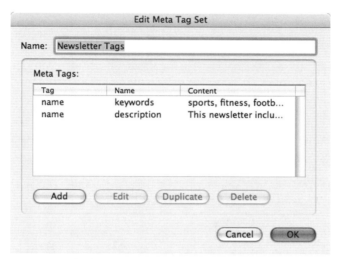

FIGURE 12.21 In this example a meta tag set named Newsletter Tags consists of two meta tags: one for keywords and one for a description.

4. In the Edit Meta Tag dialog box (**Figure 12.22**), choose an attribute from the Meta Tag menu or enter an attribute in the Meta Tag field.

5. Choose a name from the Name menu to associate it with the meta tag type in the Meta Tag field (keywords and description are the two most commonly used).

6. Enter the content of the meta tag in the Content field.

FIGURE 12.22 The Edit Meta Tag dialog box lets you configure a meta tag, including its content. In this example, several keywords have been added to the "keywords" meta tag.

To associate a meta tag set with a Web page, choose Page > Properties, and then choose a meta tag set from the Meta Tag Set menu.

> **TIP: IMPORTING FLASH FILES**
>
> *In addition to importing pictures into Web layouts, you can also import Flash (.swf) files. When you export a Web layout as HTML, imported .swf files are copied to the folder that contains the HTML page and are displayed when the page is opened in a browser.*

Adding pages to Web layouts

Adding pages to a Web layout is exactly the same as for print layouts. You can choose Page > Insert, you can choose Insert Pages from the Pages palette menu, or you can drag master page icons into the layout page area in the Pages palette. (See Chapter 9 for information about adding, deleting, and rearranging pages.)

By default, the first page in a Web layout is named Export1, the second page is Export2, and so on. (Web pages aren't numbered like the pages in a print layout because the pages in a Web layout aren't necessarily displayed sequentially in a browser.) You can change the name of a page in a Web layout by clicking the name in the Pages palette and entering a new name.

Previewing Web layouts

Although a Web layout will probably look much the same in a browser window as it does in QuarkXPress, there will also be some differences. Different browsers can display the same Web page differently. As you work on a Web layout, you're going to want to preview the pages in a browser to see exactly what they look like in "real life."

QuarkXPress offers the following options for previewing Web pages:

- Choose a browser from the HTML Preview menu ⬛ at the bottom of the project window. If you simply click the menu, the page that's currently displayed in the project window is displayed in your computer's default browser.
- Choose Page > Preview HTML and choose a browser from the submenu.
- Choose File > Print or use the keyboard shortcut.

If you've installed a browser that is not displayed in the list of choices, you can add it by opening the Preferences dialog box, choosing Browsers in the scroll list on the left of the dialog box, and then clicking the Add button.

TIP: **DUAL-MONITOR SETUP**

Chances are, you'll frequently switch back and forth between QuarkXPress and a browser window as you work on Web layouts. If your budget and desk space allow, using a two-monitor configuration can save you a lot of time. In a two-monitor setup, you can display the Web layout on your primary monitor and preview pages in a browser on the secondary monitor.

Exporting Web layouts

When you finish a Web layout, you must export the pages in HTML format so that they can be opened and viewed with a Web browser. To export a Web layout as HTML:

1. Choose File > Export > HTML or click the Export button ⬛ at the bottom of the project window and choose HTML from the menu.

2. Click New Folder at the bottom left of the Export HTML dialog box (**Figure 12.23**), and then name and create the folder.

3. Choose an option from the Export as menu. HTML is the best option for ensuring compatibility with most browsers. Choose XHTML to create an HTML file that is also an XML file. Not all browsers support XHTML.

4. Specify the pages you want to export in the Pages field. (The default setting is All.)

5. Select an option from the Encoding menu. If the layout includes fonts and characters from multiple languages, choose Unicode (UTF-8); if it includes only fonts and characters from a single language, choose the corresponding entry from the menu.

6. Optional: If you want to view the first page of the layout in your default browser after export, select Launch Browser. If you want to store style information in the exported layout as a Cascading Style Sheet (CSS), check External CSS File.

FIGURE 12.23 The Export HTML dialog box. This dialog box always opens to a default location. If you don't want to use the default folder, navigate to a different location, and then click New Folder.

When you export a Web layout, the resulting HTML files are placed in a default folder unless you create a new folder during export, as explained above. Also, an additional folder named "images" is created within the folder that contains the HTML files. All of the picture files (.jpg, .gif, and .png) that are generated when you export a layout are placed within the "images" folder. You can change the default folder for exported HTML files and the default name for the folder in which exported picture files are placed. To change either, display the Web Layout > General pane in the Preferences dialog box. The name you enter in the Image Root Directory is used for the folder in which exported pictures are saved. Click the Browse button to specify the Site Root Directory. The folder you choose or create becomes the default folder for exported HTML files.

Converting layouts between print and Web

In addition to creating a project with both a print layout and a Web layout, you can also convert a print layout into a Web layout and vice versa.

The easiest way to turn a print layout into a Web layout is to duplicate the print layout by choosing Layout > Duplicate. This displays the Duplicate Layout dialog box, which is identical to the New Layout dialog box. Choose Web from the Layout Type menu to convert the duplicate layout into a Web layout.

When you convert a print layout into a Web layout, Convert to Graphic on Export is checked (in the Modify dialog box) for all text boxes. If you want, you can uncheck this option for individual text boxes to export them as HTML text boxes rather than pictures. If you don't check Convert to Graphic on Export, tabs are converted to word spaces.

You can also use the method described above (Layout > Duplicate) to convert a Web layout into a print layout. When you convert a Web layout into a print layout, HTML form boxes and form elements are deleted, rollovers and image maps are converted into standard picture boxes, and all text boxes (HTML text boxes and rasterized text boxes) are converted into standard text boxes.

CHAPTER 13

Flash

QUARKXPRESS 8 HAS THREE TYPES OF LAYOUTS: PRINT, WEB, AND INTERACTIVE. Interactive layouts—which may contain movies, animations, and sounds—can be exported as SWF files for display with the Adobe Flash Player. (The Flash Player is a free program that helps Web browsers display interactive content on Mac or Windows.) Experienced multimedia programmers create Flash files in Adobe Flash CS4 Professional.

QuarkXPress 8 frees designers from the need to be programmers by providing familiar tools for creating interactive online content. You can start an interactive project from scratch; share content among print, Web, and interactive layouts; or use converted print or Web content as a starting point for an interactive layout destined for Flash export. Flash files are often built into Web sites or distributed on CD. This chapter provides a quick introduction to the interactive layout features for designers interested in pursuing Flash.

In this chapter you'll learn how to create an interactive layout, where the basic controls are, and how to preview and export a Flash file.

Understanding interactive layouts

Creating an interactive layout within a project is easy. Developing multimedia content for the layout, planning the user interaction, and then pulling it all together in QuarkXPress, however, is more of a challenge. The resources, skills, and time involved include:

- **Multimedia files:** Although you can create some buttons and other interactive pieces in QuarkXPress, presentations can be more compelling if you integrate sound, video, and animations. This means you need to create or legally acquire some multimedia files.

- **Plan of interaction:** To make the best use of the media, you need a plan. As with print, start with the goal. What are you trying to communicate? How will the user interact with the piece? Do you need to collect information from the user? You may want to create a flow chart or thumbnails of pages.

- **The building blocks:** The interactive layout will generally combine multimedia files with QuarkXPress objects and planned interactivity. The process of converting simple QuarkXPress items into interactive objects such as buttons and menus is nonintuitive and somewhat cumbersome. Give yourself time to learn the features and experiment with different options.

Quark is selling the process as "easy," but that means easy for a designer when compared to programming. With planning and time, however, you can learn the interactive features in QuarkXPress 8 and offer your company or your clients an entirely new option for communication. In fact, a marketing company in Denver used the predecessor to interactive layouts, an XTension to QuarkXPress 7 called Quark Interactive Designer, to create an online catalog of its own work. During every photo shoot and interview for print content, the company produced video and sound files to enliven the content on the Web. The catalog layout already existed in QuarkXPress, so a designer converted the print layout to interactive, plugged in the multimedia files, and added interactive features. A designer with no programming skills managed to learn the software and convert an 86-page print catalog to a dynamic, browser-size Flash piece in about a week—an estimated 50% time savings over programming.

Once the first two pieces are in place—the multimedia and the plan—you can jump into QuarkXPress and create an interactive layout.

To read more about how to fit Flash creation into a real-world workflow, visit www.quark.com/products/interactivedesigner/success.html. This story illustrates how companies can save time and money while increasing their business using the interactivity features built into QuarkXPress.

Creating an interactive layout

You have several options for creating an interactive layout:

- **Create a new project and layout:** To create a new project that contains an interactive layout, choose File > New > Layout. In the New Project dialog box, choose Interactive from the Layout Type menu (**Figure 13.1**). For a Flash project, be sure that Interactive Type is set to Presentation. (The other two types, Image Sequence and Button, are used within interactive presentation layouts.)

- **Add a layout to an existing project:** If you're working already working in a project that contains a print or Web layout, you can add an interactive layout by choosing Layout > New.

- **Duplicate an existing layout and convert it:** To reuse portions of an existing layout as the starting point for an interactive layout, choose Layout > Duplicate. In the Duplicate Layout dialog box, choose Interactive for the Layout Type and rename the layout.

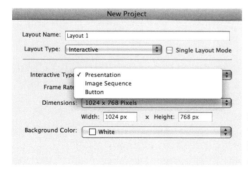

FIGURE 13.1: Choose Interactive from the Layout Type menu to create a new interactive layout or to convert a print or Web layout to an interactive layout.

Designing an interactive layout

Much of designing an interactive layout is similar to designing any layout—design master pages for backgrounds, create items to contain text and pictures, and format text with character and paragraph attributes. Once you have the basic QuarkXPress look, you can start working with the three building blocks of interactive layouts: objects, user events, and actions.

- **Objects:** An object is a named item that the user interacts with.

- **User events:** A user event is what the user does with the mouse.

- **Actions:** An action is the result of the user event.

For example, a button is an object that users click in order to turn pages.

Reviewing interactive object types

In interactive layouts, QuarkXPress items are called objects. Some objects are simply standard QuarkXPress items (such as boxes and lines) that become the background for a layout. Other objects are named and have user events associated with them. The object types include: basic, button, animation, video, SWF, text box, menu, window, and button group. To work with objects, use the Object tab of the Interactive palette (Window) menu.

Building interactive layouts

The process of building interactive layouts starts with creating named objects to interact with. You then specify how the user interacts with the object and what action occurs. For example, a video object might start to play when you display its page or when you click a play button. You can see the process when importing another SWF file into an interactive presentation:

1. Create and select a picture box to contain the SWF file.

2. Choose Window > Interactive. You will use the Interactive palette to create an SWF object from the picture box and import an SWF file (**Figure 13.2**).

3. Click the Objects tab.

4. In the Name field, enter a name for the new SWF object.

5. From the Type menu, choose SWF.

6. From the SWF menu, choose "Choose." Navigate to and select an SWF file to import.

7. Use the Options and Initially At menus to specify when the SWF file plays.

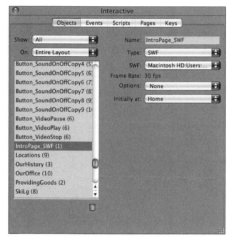

FIGURE 13.2: The Objects tab of the Interactive palette (Window menu) lists the interactive objects in the layout and lets you configure them.

The Events tab and the Scripts tab of the Interactive palette let you control how users interact with objects (**Figure 13.3**).

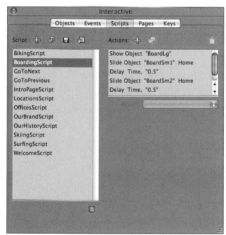

FIGURE 13.3: Use the Scripts tab to create a sequence of actions for objects.

When designing print layouts, you'll print many drafts and create many PDFs for review. It's the same with interactive presentation layouts—except you'll need to preview your work in the Adobe Flash Player to make sure what you're doing in QuarkXPress translates well to an online format. As with print layouts, you can troubleshoot preview and export issues with the Usage dialog box.

Previewing presentations

Although you can't control your users' viewing environment, it's good idea to calibrate your monitor periodically while designing interactive layouts. At least you will have more accurate color on your screen. To preview an interactive presentation layout:

- Click the SWF Preview button on the lower-right corner of the project window (Figure 13.4).

FIGURE 13.4: The SWF Preview button on the project window provides quick access to previews.

- Choose Page > Preview SWF > Preview Page or Preview Layout (**Figure 13.5**). The same command is available in the Layout menu as well.

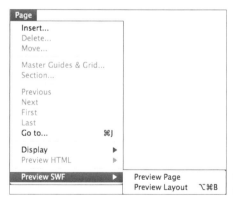

FIGURE 13.5: The Preview SWF submenu of the Page menu.

TIP **DOWNLOADING ADOBE FLASH PLAYER**

If you do not have Adobe Flash Player, visit www.adobe.com/products/flashplayer to download a free copy.

Troubleshooting multimedia files

As with picture files for print output, any multimedia files you import into an interactive presentation need to be linked to the layout for proper preview and export. To confirm the status of multimedia files:

1. Choose Utilities > Usage.

2. Click the Multimedia tab (**Figure 13.6**).

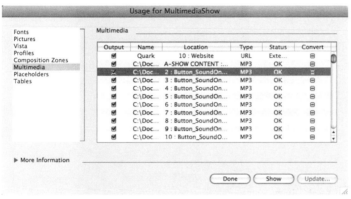

FIGURE 13.6: The Multimedia tab of the Usage dialog box (Utilities menu) lets you locate missing files and update modified files.

3. The Modified status indicates that a file has been updated since you imported it. If you're sure those changes were intentional, select each file and click Update.

4. The Missing status indicates that file has been moved since you imported it. Select each file and click Update to locate it.

5. If you suspect that a file is causing problems in a presentation, uncheck Output next to the file name. Try previewing or exporting the interactive layout to see if the presentation works without that file.

TIP **CONVERTING SOUND FILES**

Sound files can be converted to the MP3 format if necessary during export. Check Convert next to a sound file's name.

Exporting interactive layouts

Interactive presentation layouts can be exported in SWF format for display through the free stand-alone Flash Player or an embedded Flash Player. Preferences and export settings let you fine-tune the exported file for the intended media.

Exporting presentations

Before you export an interactive presentation layout, confirm the status of all imported multimedia files (Utilities > Usage > Multimedia). If each file's status is OK, you're ready to export the file. To export the active layout:

1. Choose File > Export > Exporter for Adobe® Flash® (**Figure 13.7**).

FIGURE 13.7: Customize the export of an interactive presentation layout in the Exporter for Adobe® Flash® dialog box.

2. Specify a name and location for the exported file.

3. From the Export Type menu, leave the setting at Adobe® Flash® to create an SWF file for viewing in the free Flash Player. This file can be incorporated into a Web site or viewed as a stand-alone presentation. To bundle the Flash Player into the file for either Mac or Windows, choose Macintosh Project (a Mac-only option) or Windows Projector.

4. To create a presentation that automatically expands to the size of the viewing monitor, check Export as Full Screen.

5. To customize the font handling and compression in the exported file, click Options. The controls in the Export Settings dialog box work the same as their counterparts in the SWF tab of the Preferences dialog box.

6. To export specific pages of the active layout, enter those page numbers in the Pages field.

Checking SWF preferences

The default settings for exported interactive presentation layouts are specified in the SWF tab of the Preferences dialog box (**Figure 13.8**). You can customize these settings for an exported layout as necessary by clicking Options in the Exporter for Adobe® Flash® dialog box.

TIP **PREDICTING SYSTEM SETUP**

To set options for exported SWF files, consider your average reader's system setup. Is the audience likely to have a high-speed Internet connection or dial-up? How up-to-date might are systems? If your average reader works in high-tech, for example, you can favor high quality over compression and require a higher version of the Flash Player.

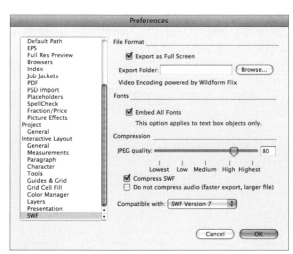

FIGURE 13.8: Set defaults for exported interactive presentation layouts in the SWF tab of the Preferences dialog box.

The controls in the SWF tab work as follows:

- **Export as Full Screen:** To create a presentation that automatically expands to the size of the viewing monitor, check Export as Full Screen.

- **Export Folder:** To browse to a default location for exported files, click Browse.

- **Embed All Fonts:** To ensure that fonts display properly in text box objects, check Embed All Fonts.

- **JPEG Quality slider:** Use the slider to control how much imported JPEGs are compressed. Higher quality creates larger file sizes that download slower; lower quality creates smaller file sizes that download quicker.

- **Compress SWF:** To compress exported SWF files, check Compress SWF. Compressed files take less time to download, but they may take slightly longer to start playing.

- **Do Not Compress Audio:** To create smaller files that are faster to download, check Do Not Compress Audio; note that the sound quality may suffer.

- **Compatible With:** To specify the minimum version of Flash Player for your presentation, choose an option from the Compatible With menu. Higher versions provide more features while lower versions can reach more viewers (as more viewers will have older versions of Flash Player).

TIP *LEARNING MORE ABOUT INTERACTIVE LAYOUTS*

You can find complete information on building interactive layouts in the QXP User Guide.pdf (QuarkXPress folder > Documents > English) along with helpful samples in the "Interactive layouts" tutorial at www.quark.com (Support > Training).

Retraining the QuarkXPress Mind

YOU'VE BEEN HUMMING ALONG WITH QUARKXPRESS ALL THESE YEARS, spending more time with it than with your friends and family, pumping out document after project after layout as the software is updated. You barely have time to keep up with your work, much less learn new features. If this sounds like you, a glance at QuarkXPress 8 might be stressful. What happened to the tools? What's going on with my old friend the Measurements palette? Not to worry—everything you need is there, and it's easier to use than ever before.

Think about when you're renting a car. You know how to drive, but you may not know how to operate the headlights, windshield wipers, GPS, and the like on the car you're renting. Customer service representatives at the nicer car rental agencies show you how these necessities work. You may have to figure out the radio yourself, but they'll make sure you get on the road safely. Think of this appendix as your QuarkXPress 8 customer service representative. It's not going to teach you to drive—just get you going.

In this appendix you'll learn about modifications to QuarkXPress since version 7.2, including changes to the tools, document window, and Measurements palette; new ways to work; and what's new and enhanced in QuarkXPress 8.

Learning the new tools

The first thing you'll notice about QuarkXPress 8 is the radically new Tools palette (**Figure 1**). While Quark has changed the configuration of the Tools palette several times over the years, the basic tools have remained the same until now. The most significant changes involve the Content tool and the box tools. The Content tool is now split into two tools (the Text Content tool and the Picture Content tool) while the Text Box tools and Picture Box tools have been combined into plain-old box tools. Many other tools are consolidated into the familiar pop-out menus.

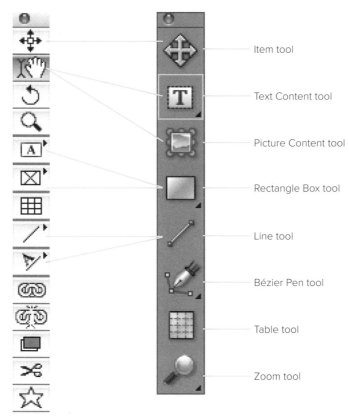

Item tool

Text Content tool

Picture Content tool

Rectangle Box tool

Line tool

Bézier Pen tool

Table tool

Zoom tool

FIGURE 1: This illustration shows how the basic item creation and item manipulation tools map to the new tools. The Item tool now allows rotation, so the Rotate tool has been removed. A new Bézier Pen tool is available at all times, while the familiar Table and Zoom tools have moved to the bottom of the Tools palette.

As with previous versions of QuarkXPress, a small black triangle on a tool indicates a pop-out menu of additional tools. Also as before, click and hold to display the tools, then drag to select one. You can now use single-letter keyboard shortcuts to select tools whether they are displayed or not. **Figure 2** shows each pop-out menu.

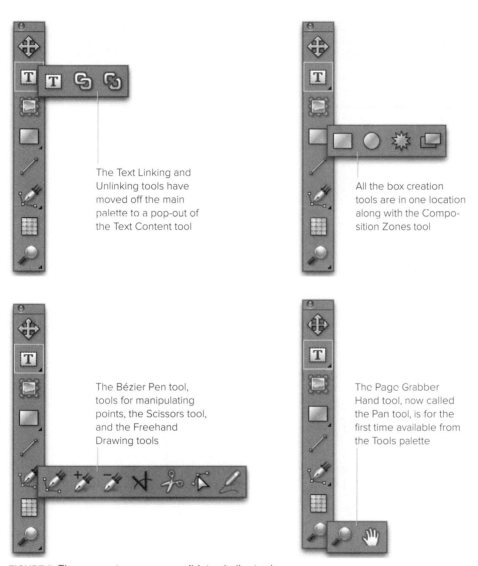

The Text Linking and Unlinking tools have moved off the main palette to a pop-out of the Text Content tool

All the box creation tools are in one location along with the Composition Zones tool

The Bézier Pen tool, tools for manipulating points, the Scissors tool, and the Freehand Drawing tools

The Page Grabber Hand tool, now called the Pan tool, is for the first time available from the Tools palette

FIGURE 2: The pop-out menus consolidate similar tools.

Selecting tools with keyboard shortcuts

QuarkXPress has always let you switch among tools with various keyboard short-cuts. Version 8, however, introduces single-letter keyboard shortcuts that are easier to remember and use. The shortcuts are often intuitive—B for box tools, for example—and can be used any time that you're not using the Text Content tool. This change is a big part of what makes using QuarkXPress 8 a more fluid design and layout experience, so give it a try. To experiment with the shortcuts, try memorizing just one and using it. Once you appreciate the difference, you'll be inspired to use them all.

- **V** (Item tool)

- **T** (Text Content tool, Text Linking tool, Text Unlinking tool)

- **R** (Picture Content tool)

- **B** (Rectangle Box tool, Oval Box tool, Star Box tool, Composition Zones tool)*

- **L** (Line tool)

- **P** (Bézier Pen tool, Add Point tool, Remove Point tool, Convert Point tool, Scissors tool, Select Point tool, Freehand Drawing tool)*

- **G** (Table tool)

- **Z** (Zoom tool)

- **X** (Pan tool)

*Within a pop-out menu of tools, different tools may have the same shortcut. Press the shortcut key repeatedly until you select the tool you want.

TIP **NEW DOG KEEPS OLD TRICKS**

The majority of your old tool-selection tricks still work—for example, you can still press Option/Alt for temporary access to the Pan tool (the tool formerly known as the Page Grabber Hand). The difference with the single-letter shortcuts is that the tool stays selected until you select another tool.

Showing tool tips

If you can't figure out which tool you need, check the names for help. Point at a tool until its tool tip displays (**Figure 3**). If it doesn't display, make sure Show Tool Tips is checked in the Input Settings tab of the Preferences dialog box (Preferences > Application > Input Settings).

FIGURE 3: When working with the new Tools palette—or any other unfamiliar control— don't forget that you can easily decipher an icon by displaying its tool tip.

The document window

The main QuarkXPress document window remains familiar, with just a few changes in the left-hand corners. First, you'll see that the tabs for each layout within the project are now in the upper-left corner rather than the lower-left corner (**Figure 4**). The lower-left corner continues to provide navigation controls, but they are greatly enhanced, as shown in **Figure 5**.

FIGURE 4: The tabs for each layout within a project are now in the upper-left corner of the document window.

Click View Master Page to jump directly to the selected item's master page Click here to split the document window horizontally or vertically

FIGURE 5: The lower-left corner of the project window provides enhanced view, navigation, and export controls. Preview controls for Web and interactive layouts display on the far right side.

The Measurements palette

The Measurements palette went through a major overhaul in version 7, which introduced tabs to consolidate various categories of formatting controls. The original structure of the Measurements palette—providing quick access to a wide variety of often-used controls—was maintained in the Classic tab. This concept is expanded in version 8 with even more controls. The tabbed Measurements palette in QuarkXPress 7 and 8 (**Figure 6**) puts almost every formatting option in QuarkXPress at your fingertips—if you can only find it and recognize it.

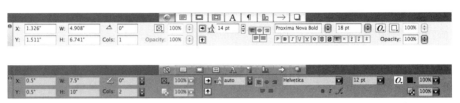

FIGURE 6: The Classic tab of the QuarkXPress Measurements palette shows the familiar controls for positioning a text box and formatting text. QuarkXPress 8 introduces minor differences such as buttons for each type style in version 7 (top) to buttons for Bold and Italic plus a Text Styles menu (bottom).

To get the most out of the new Measurements palette, consider these tips:

- **Always show the tab bar.** The tab bar displays the icons that let you switch tabs in the Measurements palette. By default, it's set to Show Tab on Rollover, which forces you to wait a fraction of a second to see the icons and pause to see their tool tips. Even on the smallest monitors, you should be able to spare the room to display the tab bar at all times—otherwise, you may forget the new controls are there. Control+click/right+click the Measurements palette title bar (the narrow vertical bar on the far left side) and Choose Always Show Tab Bar from the context menu.

- **Consult tools tips.** If anything could disprove "a picture is worth a thousand words," it would be the proliferation of palette icons in software. Half the time, you can't tell what a tool or feature does by its icon. Fortunately, as with the new tools and any other unfamiliar control in QuarkXPress, you can point at Measurements palette controls to see their actual names in tool tips. If you don't see the tool tips, be sure Show Tool Tips is checked in the Input Settings tab of the Preferences dialog box (Preferences > Application > Input Settings).

- **Continue to use the Character Attributes, Paragraph Attributes, and Modify dialog boxes.** When you're setting up basic text and item formatting, it may be easier to use a formatting dialog box. The dialog boxes provide nice, clear, named controls and they consolidate scores of options all in one place. You can then use the Measurements palette for fine tuning.

TIP **CLASSIC MEASUREMENTS PALETTE FOR LUDDITES**

Whether you're a Luddite at heart—or you give the new Measurements palette the old college try and still don't like it—you can turn back time. Display the Classic tab (click the icon on the far left side of the tab bar), then choose Always Hide Tab Bar from the palette's context menu.

Changing the way you work

Picture this: To start a new job, you drag all the text and picture files from your desktop to the page. No creating text boxes and picture boxes. No resizing the boxes to fit the content. Select some text and start choosing fonts by looking at previews in a font menu. No trip out to a font manager or type book to select typefaces. On to the pictures—check the resolution in the Measurements palette to make sure they're usable. No need to open the files in Photoshop. Use the Picture Content tool and the picture's own handles to adjust size and placement. No need to estimate percentages and offset values. For the layout, create a design grid for precision item and text positioning rather than, again, relying on X, Y values.

As you can see, QuarkXPress 8 creates a much more fluid workspace. You no longer have to stop and plan out your actions—just get the content on the page and start experimenting with it. As you work, take advantage of the ability to switch tools with a single keystroke, easily navigate among pages and layouts, and manage your palettes and windows. As you solidify a design, start making styles—paragraph style sheets, character style sheets, item styles, and grid styles—for automatic, consistent formatting. Then, when you (or your client) inevitably make changes, you can implement them globally in seconds.

To make this fantasy a reality, all you need to do is start trying out the new features of QuarkXPress 8.

What happened to...?

If you're stuck and can't find a favorite tool, check this list. The most prominent changes in QuarkXPress 8 are highlighted here.

Content tool

What happened to the Content tool? It split into two tools—the Text Content tool and the Picture Content tool. Are you going to have to switch tools all the time? Yes, but switching is easy because if you double-click in a text box, the Text Content tool is selected for you. And, unlike other programs with special-purpose tools, you can still resize boxes while working with the Text Content and Picture Content tools.

Rotate tool

Where's the Rotate tool? Gone baby, gone. You no longer need it since you can rotate items by hovering the mouse above any corner until you see the rotate pointer ↴. You can also enter values in the Angle fields available in various tabs of the Measurements palette and the Modify dialog boxes.

Text Box and Picture Box tools

Since QuarkXPress no longer requires specific box types, you no longer need special-purpose tools for creating text boxes and picture boxes. All the Text Box and Picture Box tools are now consolidated into generic box tools. You can now import text or a picture in any box.

Orthogonal Line tool

If you're missing the plus sign—aka the Orthogonal Line tool—you've been around the block with QuarkXPress. An old faithful tool, it created only horizontal or vertical lines, in case you've forgotten the definition from geometry. As you no doubt recall, you can create orthogonal lines with the Line tool by pressing Shift as you draw.

Text-Path tools

Like the Rotate tool, the Text-Path tools are obsolete in QuarkXPress 8. You can now click on any item with the Text Content tool and start typing. Therefore, you no longer need to create specific paths to contain text.

Linking and Unlinking tools

Are the Linking and Unlinking tools gone? No. They're tucked inside a pop-out menu of the Text Content tool. If you're not working with text, you can press T on the keyboard until the one you need is selected. And guess what—now that tool stays selected until you're finished using it. In previous versions of QuarkXPress, you had to Option/Alt-click the tool to keep it selected.

Polygon tool

The tools for creating polygon text and picture boxes are gone but not forgotten. A sentimental favorite since they were introduced in version 3—designers were no longer restricted to circles and squares!—hopefully the polygon tools will return someday. In the meantime, you'll have to fumble along with the drawing tools and the Starburst tool.

Corner box tools

If you were a big fan of actually drawing concave-corner boxes, you are out of luck. Fortunately, all you need to do now is create a rectangular box and choose a Corner Style from the Box tab of the Modify dialog box (Item menu). The beauty of corner styles as a box attribute—aside from clearing clutter from the Tools palette—is that the corner style can be saved with an item style (Edit > Item Styles) and altered with search and replace (Edit > Item Find/Change).

Space/Align dialog box

The Space/Align dialog box was replaced with the Space/Align tab of the Measurements palette in version 7, but you may still miss it in version 8. You should find that the Space/Align icons are more intuitive than the old method.

New features and enhancements

Once you get accustomed to using QuarkXPress 8, start taking advantage of all the new features and enhanced capabilities. Some of these features were available in free XTensions for QuarkXPress 7, but they are now shipping with the software for all users.

- **Drag and drop.** One of the coolest features in QuarkXPress 8 is the ability to drag text and picture files from your desktop or another program into a layout. The three-step process of creating a box, locating the file, and importing it are no longer necessary. You can also drag text and pictures from QuarkXPress to the desktop or to another application.

- **Interactive layouts.** Use familiar QuarkXPress tools plus the features of the bundled Quark Interactive Designer XTension to design Flash files (Layout > New > Layout Type > Interactive). You can share content among print, Web, and interactive layouts within a project.

- **Picture resolution on display.** You can now see the effective picture resolution of the selected picture in the Measurements palette—a tiny feature that can save you endless time and hassle. See the Effective Image Resolution field 318.3 dpi in the lower-right corner of the Classic tab.

- **Hanging punctuation.** Designers often want to "hang" punctuation or other characters outside the text margin for a smoother look. You can apply default settings through the Formats tab of the Paragraph Attributes dialog box (Style menu) and create your own hanging character sets (Edit > Hanging Characters).

- **Design grids and grid styles.** Choose Window > Grid Styles, then choose New from the palette menu to see all the new features for creating baseline grids. You can create a sophisticated grid for positioning items and text and specify custom colors for the various guides. Grids are saved as styles to apply to master pages and individual text boxes.

- **Guide controls.** The bundled Guide Manager Pro XTension gives you complete control over the creation, placement, color, and display of guides, and lets you lock guides (Window > Guides).

- **Duplicate items with the mouse.** When an item is selected with the item tool, you can duplicate it by dragging it, then pressing Option (Mac) or Alt (Windows) before you release the mouse button. The original item stays in place.

- **Resize items from the center.** You can now resize an item from its center by pressing Option (Mac) or Alt (Windows) as you drag a resize handle.

- **Item styles.** The scores of formatting attributes you can apply to items can now be bundled into styles, which you can apply with one click (Window > Item Styles). As you'd expect, updates to styles affect all items to which the style is applied.

- **Item Find/Change.** You can now search and replace any combination of item formatting attributes (Edit > Item Find/Change). For example, if you need to change all 1-point cyan rules to .25 point magenta rules, you can do it in one quick operation.

- **WYSIWYG font menus.** At long last, QuarkXPress now displays previews of fonts in all font menus. While this is handy if you don't know what all your fonts look like, it can take a little time if you have hundreds of fonts active on your system. Fortunately, you can turn it off temporarily by pressing Shift when you click a font menu or by unchecking Show in Font Menu in the Fonts tab of the Preferences dialog box. When Show in Font Menu is unchecked, you can display previews by Shift+clicking a font menu.

- **Improved drawing tools.** The new Bézier Pen tool and accompanying editing tools now function more like those in standard illustration programs.

- **Update style sheets.** Like most programs, QuarkXPress now lets you update a style sheet based on formatted text. Select the text and click the Update button on the Paragraph or Character portion of the Style Sheets palette.

- **Spell checking preferences.** The SpellCheck tab in the Preferences dialog box lets you check Ignore Words With Numbers and Ignore Internet and File Addresses to speed up the spell-check process.

- **Text-to-box expanded.** QuarkXPress 4 introduced the ability to select a line of text and convert it to a box to contain more text or a picture. The limitation of a "line" is now gone and you can convert all the selected text you want (Item > Convert Text to Boxes). In addition, you can now decide whether the converted text is anchored in text or not.

- **Universal file format for major languages.** Users can now open documents created in any language's version of QuarkXPress 8, including East Asian versions. Improved Font Fallback helps with missing fonts from various languages.

- **PDF and Illustrator support.** Import pictures in native Illustrator 8 and later formats and PDF 1.6 and 1.7 formats.